FORWARD/COMMENTARY

The National Institute of Standards and Technology (NIST) is a measurement standards laboratory, and a non-regulatory agency of the United States Department of Commerce. Its mission is to promote innovation and industrial competitiveness. Founded in 1901, as the National Bureau of Standards, NIST was formed with the mandate to provide standard weights and measures, and to serve as the national physical laboratory for the United States. With a world-class measurement and testing laboratory encompassing a wide range of areas of computer science, mathematics, statistics, and systems engineering, NIST's cybersecurity program supports its overall mission to promote U.S. innovation and industrial competitiveness by advancing measurement science, standards, and related technology through research and development in ways that enhance economic security and improve our quality of life.

The need for cybersecurity standards and best practices that address interoperability, usability and privacy has been shown to be critical for the nation. NIST's cybersecurity programs seek to enable greater development and application of practical, innovative security technologies and methodologies that enhance the country's ability to address current and future computer and information security challenges.

The cybersecurity publications produced by NIST cover a wide range of cybersecurity concepts that are carefully designed to work together to produce a holistic approach to cybersecurity primarily for government agencies and constitute the best practices used by industry. This holistic strategy to cybersecurity covers the gamut of security subjects from development of secure encryption standards for communication and storage of information while at rest to how best to recover from a cyber-attack.

Why buy a book you can download for free?   We print this so you don't have to.

Some are available only in electronic media. Some online docs are missing pages or barely legible.

We at 4th Watch Publishing are former government employees, so we know how government employees actually use the standards. When a new standard is released, an engineer prints it out, punches holes and puts it in a 3-ring binder. While this is not a big deal for a 5 or 10-page document, many NIST documents are over 100 pages and printing a large document is a time-consuming effort. So, an engineer that's paid $75 an hour is spending hours simply printing out the tools needed to do the job. That's time that could be better spent doing engineering. We publish these documents so engineers can focus on what they were hired to do – engineering. It's much more cost-effective to just order the latest version from Amazon.com

If there is a standard you would like published, let us know. Our web site is usgovpub.com

Many of our titles are available as eBooks for Kindle, iPad, Nook, remarkable, BOOX, and Sony eReaders. Buy the paperback from Amazon and get Kindle eBook FREE using MATCHBOOK. Go to https://usgovpub.com to learn more.

Why buy an eBook when you can access data on a website for free? HYPERLINKS

Yes, many books are available as a PDF, but not all PDFs are bookmarked? Do you really want to search a 6,500-page PDF document manually? Load our copy onto your Kindle, PC, iPad, Android Tablet, Nook, or iPhone (download the FREE kindle App from the APP Store) and you have an easily searchable copy. Most devices will allow you to easily navigate an ePub to any Chapter. Note that there is a distinction between a Table of Contents and "Page Navigation". Page Navigation refers to a different sort of Table of Contents. Not one appearing as a page in the book, but one that shows up on the device itself when the reader accesses the navigation feature. Readers can click on a navigation link to jump to a Chapter or Subchapter. Once there, most devices allow you to "pinch and zoom" in or out to easily read the text. (Unfortunately, downloading the free sample file at Amazon.com does not include this feature. You have to buy a copy to get that functionality, but as inexpensive as eBooks are, it's worth it.) Kindle allows you to do word search and Page Flip (temporary place holder takes you back when you want to go back and check something). Visit **USGOVPUB.COM** to learn more.

DRAFT NISTIR 8183A
Volume 1

Cybersecurity Framework Manufacturing Profile Low Security Level Example Implementations Guide:
Volume 1 – General Implementation Guidance

Keith Stouffer
Timothy Zimmerman
CheeYee Tang
Jeffrey Cichonski
Neeraj Shah
Wesley Downard

This publication is available free of charge from:
https://doi.org/10.6028/NIST.IR.8183A-1-draft

National Institute of
Standards and Technology
U.S. Department of Commerce

DRAFT NISTIR 8183A
Volume 1

Cybersecurity Framework Manufacturing Profile Low Security Level Example Implementations Guide:
Volume 1 – General Implementation Guidance

Keith Stouffer
Timothy Zimmerman
CheeYee Tang
Intelligent Systems Division
Engineering Laboratory

Neeraj Shah
Strativia, LLC
Largo, Maryland

Jeffrey Cichonski
Applied Cybersecurity Division
Information Technology Laboratory

Wesley Downard
G2, Inc.
Annapolis Junction, Maryland

This publication is available free of charge from:
https://doi.org/10.6028/NIST.IR.8183A-1-draft

May 2019

U.S. Department of Commerce
Wilbur L. Ross, Jr., Secretary

National Institute of Standards and Technology
Walter Copan, NIST Director and Under Secretary of Commerce for Standards and Technology

National Institute of Standards and Technology Internal Report 8183A, Volume 1
80 pages (May 2019)

This publication is available free of charge from:
https://doi.org/10.6028/NIST.IR.8183A-1-draft

Public comment period: *May 28, 2019* through *July 8, 2019*

National Institute of Standards and Technology
Attn: Applied Cybersecurity Division, Information Technology Laboratory
100 Bureau Drive (Mail Stop 2000) Gaithersburg, MD 20899-2000
Email: CSF_Manufacturing_Profile_Implementation@nist.gov

All comments are subject to release under the Freedom of Information Act (FOIA).

80 **Abstract**

81 This guide provides general implementation guidance (Volume 1) and example proof-of-concept
82 solutions demonstrating how open-source and commercial off-the-shelf (COTS) products that are
83 currently available today can be implemented in manufacturing environments to satisfy the
84 requirements in the Cybersecurity Framework (CSF) Manufacturing Profile Low Security Level.
85 Example proof-of-concept solutions with measured network, device, and operational
86 performance impacts for a process-based manufacturing environment (Volume 2) and a discrete-
87 based manufacturing environment (Volume 3) are included in the guide. Depending on factors
88 like size, sophistication, risk tolerance, and threat landscape, manufacturers should make their
89 own determinations about the breadth of the proof-of-concept solutions they may voluntarily
90 implement. The CSF Manufacturing Profile can be used as a roadmap for managing
91 cybersecurity risk for manufacturers and is aligned with manufacturing sector goals and industry
92 best practices. The Manufacturing Profile provides a voluntary, risk-based approach for
93 managing cybersecurity activities and cyber risk to manufacturing systems. The Manufacturing
94 Profile is meant to compliment but not replace current cybersecurity standards and industry
95 guidelines that the manufacturer is embracing.

96

97 **Keywords**

98 Computer security; Cybersecurity Framework (CSF); distributed control systems (DCS);
99 industrial control systems (ICS); information security; manufacturing; network security;
100 programmable logic controllers (PLC); risk management; security controls; supervisory control
101 and data acquisition (SCADA) systems.

102 **Supplemental Content**

103 Additional volumes of this publication include:

104 Draft NISTIR 8183A Volume 2, *Cybersecurity Framework Manufacturing Profile Low*
105 *Security Level Example Implementations Guide: Volume 2 – Process-based*
106 *Manufacturing System Use Case.* https://doi.org/10.6028/NIST.IR.8183A-2-draft

107 Draft NISTIR 8183A Volume 3, *Cybersecurity Framework Manufacturing Profile Low*
108 *Security Level Example Implementations Guide: Volume 3 – Discrete-based*
109 *Manufacturing System Use Case.* https://doi.org/10.6028/NIST.IR.8183A-3-draft

Acknowledgments

The authors gratefully acknowledge and appreciate the significant contributions from individuals and organizations in the public and private sectors, whose thoughtful and constructive comments improved the overall quality, thoroughness, and usefulness of this publication. A special acknowledgement to the members of the ISA99, Industrial Automation and Control Systems Security Committee and the Department of Homeland Security Industrial Control System Joint Working Group (ICSJWG) for their exceptional contributions to this publication.

Note to Reviewers

This guide does not describe the solution, but a possible solution. This is a draft guide. We seek feedback on its contents and welcome your input. Comments, suggestions, and success stories will improve subsequent versions of this guide. Please contribute your thoughts to CSF_Manufacturing_Profile_Implementation@nist.gov.

Call for Patent Claims

This public review includes a call for information on essential patent claims (claims whose use would be required for compliance with the guidance or requirements in this Information Technology Laboratory (ITL) draft publication). Such guidance and/or requirements may be directly stated in this ITL Publication or by reference to another publication. This call also includes disclosure, where known, of the existence of pending U.S. or foreign patent applications relating to this ITL draft publication and of any relevant unexpired U.S. or foreign patents.

ITL may require from the patent holder, or a party authorized to make assurances on its behalf, in written or electronic form, either:

a) assurance in the form of a general disclaimer to the effect that such party does not hold and does not currently intend holding any essential patent claim(s); or

b) assurance that a license to such essential patent claim(s) will be made available to applicants desiring to utilize the license for the purpose of complying with the guidance or requirements in this ITL draft publication either:

> i) under reasonable terms and conditions that are demonstrably free of any unfair discrimination; or
>
> ii) without compensation and under reasonable terms and conditions that are demonstrably free of any unfair discrimination.

Such assurance shall indicate that the patent holder (or third party authorized to make assurances on its behalf) will include in any documents transferring ownership of patents subject to the assurance, provisions sufficient to ensure that the commitments in the assurance are binding on the transferee, and that the transferee will similarly include appropriate provisions in the event of future transfers with the goal of binding each successor-in-interest.

The assurance shall also indicate that it is intended to be binding on successors-in-interest regardless of whether such provisions are included in the relevant transfer documents.

Such statements should be addressed to: CSF_Manufacturing_Profile_Implementation@nist.gov

Table of Contents

Executive Summary

This guide provides general implementation guidance (Volume 1) and example proof-of-concept solutions demonstrating how open-source and commercial off-the-shelf (COTS) products that are currently available today can be implemented in manufacturing environments to satisfy the requirements in the Cybersecurity Framework (CSF) Manufacturing Profile [8] Low Security Level. Example proof-of-concept solutions with measured network, device, and operational performance impacts for a process-based manufacturing environment (Volume 2) and a discrete-based manufacturing environment (Volume 3) are included in the guide. Depending on factors like size, sophistication, risk tolerance, and threat landscape, manufacturers should make their own determinations about the breadth of the proof-of-concept solutions they may voluntarily implement.

The CSF Manufacturing Profile can be used as a roadmap for managing cybersecurity risk for manufacturers and is aligned with manufacturing sector goals and industry best practices. The Manufacturing Profile provides a voluntary, risk-based approach for managing cybersecurity activities and cyber risk to manufacturing systems. The Manufacturing Profile is meant to compliment but not replace current cybersecurity standards and industry guidelines that the manufacturer is embracing.

The CSF Manufacturing Profile focuses on desired cybersecurity outcomes and can be used as a roadmap to identify opportunities for improving the current cybersecurity posture of the manufacturing system. The Manufacturing Profile provides a prioritization of security activities to meet specific business/mission goals. Relevant and actionable security practices that can be implemented to support key business/mission goals are then identified.

While the proof-of-concept solutions in this guide used a suite of commercial products, this guide does not endorse these particular products, nor does it guarantee compliance with any regulatory initiatives. Your organization's information security experts should identify the products that will best integrate with your existing tools and manufacturing system infrastructure. Your organization may voluntarily adopt these solutions or one that adheres to these guidelines in whole, or you can use this guide as a starting point for tailoring and implementing parts of a solution. This guide does not describe regulations or mandatory practices, nor does it carry any statutory authority.

249 **1.   Introduction**

250   The Executive Order 13636, "Improving Critical Infrastructure Cybersecurity," [1] directed the
251   development of the voluntary Cybersecurity Framework that provides a prioritized, flexible,
252   repeatable, performance-based, and cost-effective approach to manage cybersecurity risk [1] for
253   those processes, information, and systems directly involved in the delivery of critical
254   infrastructure services.

255   The Cybersecurity Framework is a voluntary risk-based assemblage of industry standards and
256   best practices designed to help organizations manage cybersecurity risks [2]. The Framework,
257   created through collaboration between government and the private sector, uses a common
258   language to address and manage cybersecurity risk in a cost-effective way based on business
259   needs without imposing additional regulatory requirements.

260   To address the needs of manufactures, a Manufacturing Profile [8] of the Cybersecurity
261   Framework was developed, through collaboration between government and the private sector, to
262   be an actionable approach for implementing cybersecurity controls into a manufacturing system
263   and its environment. The Profile defines specific cybersecurity activities and outcomes for the
264   protection of the manufacturing system, its components, facility, and environment. Through use
265   of the Profile, the manufacturer can align cybersecurity activities with business requirements,
266   risk tolerances, and resources. The Profile provides a manufacturing sector-specific approach to
267   cybersccurity from standards, guidelines, and industry best practices.

268   **1.1   Purpose and Scope**

269   Many small and medium sized manufacturers have expressed that they are challenged in
270   implementing a standards-based cybersecurity program. This guide provides example proof-of-
271   concept solutions demonstrating how open-source and commercial off-the-shelf (COTS)
272   products that are available today can be implemented in manufacturing environments to satisfy
273   the requirements in the Cybersecurity Framework (CSF) Manufacturing Profile Low Security
274   Level. Example proof-of-concept solutions with measured network, device, and operational
275   performance impacts for a process-based manufacturing environment (Volume 2) and a discrete-
276   based manufacturing environment (Volume 3) are included in the guide. Depending on factors
277   like size, sophistication, risk tolerance, and threat landscape, manufacturers should make their
278   own determinations about the breadth of the proof-of-concept solutions they may voluntarily
279   implement. The CSF Manufacturing Profile can be used as a roadmap for managing
280   cybersecurity risk for manufacturers and is aligned with manufacturing sector goals and industry
281   best practices. The Manufacturing Profile provides a voluntary, risk-based approach for
282   managing cybersecurity activities and cyber risk to manufacturing systems. The Manufacturing
283   Profile is meant to enhance but not replace current cybersecurity standards and industry
284   guidelines that the manufacturer is embracing.

285   While the proof-of-concept solutions in this guide used a suite of commercial products, this
286   guide does not endorse these particular products, nor does it guarantee compliance with any
287   regulatory initiatives. Your organization's information security experts should identify the
288   products that will best integrate with your existing tools and manufacturing system
289   infrastructure. Organizations may voluntarily adopt these solutions or one that adheres to these
290   guidelines in whole, or can use this guide as a starting point for tailoring and implementing parts

291 of a solution. This guide does not describe regulations or mandatory practices, nor does it carry
292 any statutory authority.

293 This project is guided by the following assumptions: The solutions were developed in a lab
294 environment. The environment is based on a typical small manufacture's environment. The
295 environment does not reflect the complexity of a production environment. An organization can
296 access the skills and resources required to implement a manufacturing cybersecurity solution.

297 **1.2 Audience**

298 This document covers details specific to manufacturing systems. Readers of this document
299 should be acquainted with operational technology, general computer security concepts, and
300 communication protocols such as those used in networking. The intended audience is varied and
301 includes the following:

302 • Control engineers, integrators, and architects who design or implement secure
303   manufacturing systems.
304 • System administrators, engineers, and other information technology (IT) professionals
305   who administer, patch, or secure manufacturing systems.
306 • Managers who are responsible for manufacturing systems.
307 • Senior management who are trying to understand implications and consequences as they
308   justify and implement a manufacturing systems cybersecurity program to help mitigate
309   impacts to business functionality.
310 • Researchers, academic institutions and analysts who are trying to understand the unique
311   security needs of manufacturing systems.

312 **1.3 Document Structure**

313 The remainder of Volume 1 is divided into the following major sections:

314 • Section 2 provides an overview of manufacturing systems.
315 • Section 3 provides an overview of the CSF Manufacturing Profile
316 • Section 4 discusses the project's CSF Manufacturing Profile implementation approach.
317 • Section 5 provides an overview of the policy/procedures documents needed to meet the
318   requirements specified in CSF Manufacturing Profile Low Security Level.
319 • Section 6 provides of the technical capabilities needed to meet the requirements specified
320   in CSF Manufacturing Profile Low Security Level.
321 • Section 7 examines potential solutions that can address the requirements specified in each
322   Subcategory
323 • Section 8 provides an overview of the laboratory environment used for implementations
324 • Appendix A provides a list of acronyms and abbreviations used in this document.
325 • Appendix B provides a glossary of terms used in this document.
326 • Appendix C provides a list of references used in the development of this document.

327 Volume 2 of this guide provides a proof-of-concept CSF Manufacturing Profile Low Security
328 Level implementation for a process-based manufacturing system.

329 Volume 3 of this guide provides a proof-of-concept CSF Manufacturing Profile Low Security
330 Level implementation for a discrete-based manufacturing system.

2.　Overview of Manufacturing Systems

Manufacturing is a large and diverse industrial sector. Manufacturing industries can be categorized as either *process-based, discrete-based,* or a combination of both [3].

Process-based manufacturing industries typically utilize two main process types:

- **Continuous Manufacturing Processes.** These processes run continuously, often with phases to make different grades of a product. Typical continuous manufacturing processes include fuel or steam flow in a power plant, petroleum in a refinery, and distillation in a chemical plant.
- **Batch Manufacturing Processes.** These processes have distinct processing steps, conducted on a quantity of material. There is a distinct start and end to a batch process with the possibility of brief steady state operations during intermediate steps. Typical batch manufacturing processes include food, beverage, and biotech manufacturing.

Discrete-based manufacturing industries typically conduct a series of operations on a product to create the distinct end product. Electronic and mechanical parts assembly and parts machining are typical examples of this type of industry. Both process-based and discrete-based industries utilize similar types of control systems, sensors, and networks. Some facilities are a hybrid of discrete and process-based manufacturing.

Manufacturing industries are usually located within a confined factory or plant-centric area. Communications in manufacturing industries are typically performed using fieldbus and local area network (LAN) technologies that are reliable and high speed. Wireless networking technologies are gaining popularity in manufacturing industries. Fieldbus includes, for example, DeviceNet, Modbus, and Controller Area Network (CAN) bus.

The Manufacturing sector of the critical infrastructure community includes public and private owners and operators, along with other entities operating in the manufacturing domain. Members of the distinct critical infrastructure sector perform functions that are supported by industrial control systems (ICS) and by information technology (IT). This reliance on technology, communication, and the interconnectivity of ICS and IT has changed and expanded the potential vulnerabilities and increased potential risk to manufacturing system operations.

359 | **3.   CSF Manufacturing Profile Overview**

360 The Manufacturing Profile [8] was developed to be an actionable approach for implementing
361 cybersecurity controls into a manufacturing system and its environment. The specific statements
362 in the subcategories in Section 7 of the Manufacturing Profile were derived from the security
363 controls of the NIST SP 800-53 Rev.4 [4], and are customized to the manufacturing domain
364 using relevant informative references. The general informative references of ISA/IEC 62443 [5]
365 from the Framework are also listed in the References column. COBIT 5 is sourced for
366 subcategories that have no corresponding 800-53 references. Additional input came from NIST
367 SP 800-82, Rev. 2, both in section 6.2 (Guidance on the Application of Security Controls to ICS)
368 and in Appendix G (ICS Overlay) [3]. For informative references to an entire control family, or
369 set of controls (such as subcategory ID.GV-1's informative reference to all "policy and
370 procedures" controls), the approach took a holistic view of the controls comprising the
371 family/set.

372 The Manufacturing Profile expresses tailored values for cybersecurity controls for the
373 manufacturing system environment. These represent the application of the Categories and
374 Subcategories from the Framework based on domain-specific relevance, business drivers, risk
375 assessment, and the manufacturer's priorities. Users of the Profile can also add Categories and
376 Subcategories as needed to address unique and specific risks.

377 **4.   CSF Manufacturing Profile Implementation Approach**

378 Meeting the Manufacturing Profile subcategory requirements can be accomplished by
379 developing and implementing policies and procedures and/or implementing technical solutions,
380 depending on the particular subcategory language.

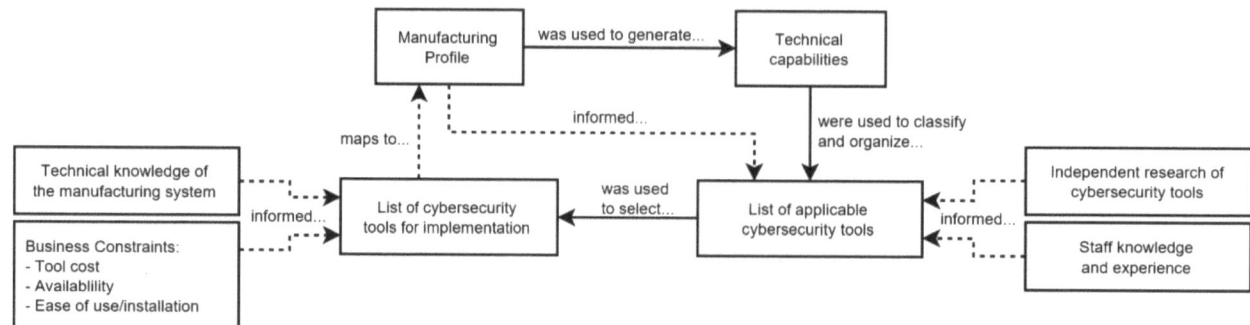

381

382   **Figure 4-1. Approach used for identifying, planning and implementing technical cybersecurity capabilities**

383 Figure 4-1 provides a visual representation of the approach used for identifying, planning and
384 implementing technical cybersecurity capabilities as well as identifying the complementing
385 cybersecurity processes and procedures. 'NISTIR 8183 Cybersecurity Framework
386 Manufacturing Profile' was the principal resource describing the cybersecurity outcomes desired
387 in both of NIST's manufacturing test bed scenarios. The outcomes described in NISTIR 8183 are
388 grounded by and cross referenced with prescriptive cybersecurity controls from standards
389 relevant to the industrial control system owners and operators.

390 The initial step of this planning process was focused on gaining an understanding of what
391 cybersecurity related tools, configurations, and best practices are required to achieve the specific
392 outcomes or profile subcategories. The profile subcategories and specific language provided by
393 mapped cybersecurity controls provided insight into classifications of technical capabilities
394 needed to be implemented in the test bed environments. From these high-level classifications of
395 capabilities, NIST researchers identified and built a list of commercial products and open source
396 tools that fit into each of these classifications. The list of solutions was then used to inform
397 implementation planning and specific solutions, tools, and products were selected for
398 implementation in the testbed environment. The selection of these technologies for
399 implementation was informed by; technical knowledge of the test bed, solution cost, availability,
400 maturity, level of expertise required for implementation and management, and the lab IT
401 administrator's expertise.

402 The mapping of technical solutions to profile subcategories in most cases did not provide exact
403 one to one coverage for achieving a profile subcategory outcome. In most scenarios, during the
404 planning process there was a realization that implementing one technical capability might only
405 satisfy portions of multiple subcategories and in some scenarios implementation of multiple
406 technical capabilities were required in order to achieve the outcome described by a profile
407 subcategory. Some profile subcategories required the implementation of a technical capability
408 complemented by the addition of a cybersecurity policy or procedure. While this mapping adds
409 complexity to the planning process it enables system owners to gain an understanding of what

410 technical solutions will enable them to achieve the most subcategory outcomes. Priorities can be
411 assigned based the specific mission and business objectives of the organization.

412 An overview of the cybersecurity policy and procedures is provided in the six documents
413 provided in Section 5.

414 An overview of technical capabilities is provided in Section 6.

5.   Policy/Procedural Capabilities Overview

For the implementation of these two use cases, 6 policy and procedural documents were produced for each:

5.1   Security Program Document

The Information Security Program document establishes guidelines and principles for initiating, implementing, maintaining, and improving information security management of the Organization. It is a documented set of the organization's security policies, procedures, guidelines and standards. The program is intended to protect the confidentiality, integrity and availability of information resources.

5.2   Security Policy Document

The Security Policy document defines the security requirements for the proper and secure use of the Information Technology services in the organization. Its goal is to protect the organization and its users to the maximum extent possible against security threats that could jeopardize their integrity, privacy, reputation, and business outcomes.

5.3   Standard Operating Procedures Document

The Standard Operating Procedures document contains step-by-step instructions to allow organization's employees carry out routine operations. Employees should complete them in the exact same way every time so that the business can remain consistent. Standard operating procedures help maintain safety and efficiency for production, operations, legal and financial departments.

5.4   Risk Management Document

The Risk Management document defines how risks associated with the organization will be identified, analyzed, and managed. It outlines the Risk Management approach for the organization. In addition, it provides standard terminology, clear roles and responsibilities and details of risk management process. This document can be used by the management to understand risks, estimate impacts, and define responses to issues. It is designed to guide the project team and stakeholders.

5.5   Incident Response Plan Document

The Incident Response Plan document describes the plan for responding to information security incidents within an organization. It defines the roles and responsibilities of participants, characterization of incidents, relationships to other policies and procedures, and reporting requirements. The purpose of this plan is to detect and react to security incidents, determine their scope and risk, respond appropriately to the incident, communicate the results and risk to all stakeholders, and reduce the likelihood of the incident from reoccurring

451 **5.6   Incident Recovery Plan Document**

452 The Incident Recovery Plan is designed to ensure the continuation of vital business processes in
453 the event that information security incident occurs. Its purpose is to inventory all of the
454 infrastructure and capture information relevant to the organization's ability to recover its IT/OT
455 environment from a cybersecurity incident.
456
457 This plan has been developed to accomplish the following objectives:
458 • Limit the magnitude of any loss by minimizing the duration of a critical application service
459   interruption.
460 • Assess damage, repair the damage, and activate the repaired computer center.
461 • Manage the recovery operation in an organized and effective manner.
462 • Prepare technology personnel to respond effectively in incident recovery situations.

463 **6.   Technical Capabilities Overview**

464 This section discusses the technical capabilities identified by the team necessary to meet the CSF
465 Manufacturing Profile language. For each technical capability, an overview of the capability is
466 provided, the security benefits of implementing the capability is listed, any potential system
467 impacts the capability could have on the manufacturing system are discussed, and the CSF
468 Manufacturing Profile subcategories that are addressed when the capability is implemented are
469 listed.

470 **6.1   Hardware Inventory Management**

471 A technical capability enabling a manufacturer to track computing and network devices within
472 the manufacturing system, including device details and location information.
473
474 **6.1.1   Security Benefit**

475 Hardware inventory management tools are used to track physical computing and network
476 devices within the manufacturing system, detect new or unauthorized devices, detect the removal
477 of devices, and track specific devices details. Having a complete inventory of what computing
478 and network devices exist in an environment will facilitate a comprehensive deployment of
479 cybersecurity protections.

480 **6.1.2   Potential System Impacts**

481 Hardware inventory management tools that use active scanning can potentially impact the
482 manufacturing system. Care must be taken before using these tools to identify manufacturing
483 system devices on an operational system. Impacts could be due to the nature of the information
484 or the volume of network traffic. Consider using hardware inventory tools that use active
485 scanning during planned downtime.

486 **6.1.3   Manufacturing Profile Subcategories**

487 ID.AM-1, PR.DS-3, DE.CM-7
488
489
490 **6.2   Software and Firmware Inventory Management**

491 Software and firmware inventory management tools are used to track software and firmware
492 installed within the manufacturing system computing and network devices, including
493 identification, version numbers, and location information.

494 **6.2.1   Security Benefit**

495 Software and firmware inventory management tools enable a manufacturer to track installed
496 software and firmware on systems within the manufacturing system, detect new or unauthorized
497 software, track software versions, and facilitate the remote removal of software. Some software
498 inventory tools also allow the tool to extend its scanning into the system itself (i.e. scan system
499 peripherals, installed RAM and processors, and network configurations).

6.2.2 Potential System Impacts

Software and firmware inventory management tools that use active scanning can potentially impact the manufacturing system. Care must be taken before using these tools on an operational system. Impacts could be due to the nature of the information or the volume of network traffic. Consider using software and firmware inventory management tools that use active scanning during planned downtime.

6.2.3 Manufacturing Profile Subcategories

ID.AM-2, PR.DS-3, DE.CM-7

6.3 Systems Development Lifecycle Management

Systems development lifecycle management tools enable a manufacturer to track the scope of activities associated with hardware and software components of the manufacturing system, encompassing each component's initiation, development and acquisition, implementation, operation and maintenance, and its ultimate decommissioning and disposal.

6.3.1 Security Benefit

Documenting hardware and software from the point or purchase/installed until it's been removed/decommissioned. During the SDL process new updates like firmware, bios, driver, software updates, and patches have been applied. Knowing this information through the SDL ensure better protection against known and unknown vulnerabilities and what systems and software require updating.

6.3.2 Potential System Impacts

Systems development lifecycle management tools should not impact the manufacturing system, as they are not typically installed or operated on the manufacturing system.

6.3.3 Manufacturing Profile Subcategories

PR.DS-3, PR.IP-1, PR.IP-2, PR.IP-6, DE.CM-7

6.4 Network Architecture Documentation

Network architecture documentation tools enable a manufacturer to identify, document, and diagram the interconnections between networked manufacturing system devices, corporate networks, and other external network connections.

6.4.1 Security Benefit

Detailed documentation of the manufacturing environment's network devices and interconnections is an important component of the manufacturing profiles identify stage. Similar to other inventory activities, a comprehensive understanding of the interconnections within the

536 environment is critical for the success deployment of cybersecurity controls. This information is
537 equally important for effective monitoring.
538
539 **6.4.2 Potential System Impacts**

540 Network architecture documentation tools that use automated topology discovery technologies
541 can potentially impact the manufacturing system. Care must be taken before using these tools on
542 an operational system. Impacts could be due to the nature of the information or the volume of
543 network traffic. Consider using network architecture documentation tools that use automated
544 topology discovery technologies during planned downtime. Physical inspections of network
545 connections could be used to document the network architecture, especially if the network is not
546 large or complicated.

547 **6.4.3 Manufacturing Profile Subcategories**

548 ID.AM-3, ID.AM-4
549
550
551 **6.5 Configuration Management**

552 Configuration management tools enable a manufacturer to establish and maintain the integrity of
553 manufacturing system hardware and software components by control of processes for
554 initializing, changing, monitoring, and auditing the configurations of the components throughout
555 the system development life cycle.

556 **6.5.1 Security Benefit**

557 Configuration management helps ensure that systems are deployed in a secure consistent state
558 and maintain this state throughout their lifetime. It reduces the risk of outages and security
559 breaches through improved visibility and tracking changes to the system. In addition, it results
560 in an improved experience for staff by detecting & correcting improper configurations that could
561 negatively impact performance or security.
562
563 **6.5.2 Potential System Impacts**

564 Configuration management tools can potentially impact the manufacturing system. These tools
565 transfer numerous different types of data over the manufacturing system network, as well as
566 potentially large amounts of data. These tools may also impact manufacturing system operations
567 by attempting to change configurations or manipulating active files within devices.
568
569 **6.5.3 Manufacturing Profile Subcategories**

570 ID.AM-3, ID.AM-4, PR.IP-1, PR.IP-4, PR.MA-1
571
572

573 ## 6.6 Baseline Establishment

574 Baseline establishment tools enable a manufacturer to support the management of baseline
575 configurations of the manufacturing system. The tools track information about the manufacturing
576 system components (e.g. software license information, software version numbers, HMI and other
577 ICS component applications, software, operating systems), current version numbers and patch
578 information on operating systems and applications; and configuration settings/parameters),
579 network topology, and the logical placement of those components within the system architecture.

580 ### 6.6.1 Security Benefit

581 The use of baselines is one of the methods used for implementing configuration management in
582 an automated way. When systems are deployed in a secure state with a secure baseline, they are
583 much more likely to be resistant to cybersecurity threats. Baselining results in efficient change
584 management and improves ability to recover quickly from an outage or cybersecurity incident.
585
586 ### 6.6.2 Potential System Impacts

587 Baseline establishment tools that use active scanning can potentially impact the manufacturing
588 system. Care must be taken before using these tools on an operational system. Impacts could be
589 due to the nature of the information or the volume of network traffic. Consider using baseline
590 establishment tools hardware that use active scanning during planned downtime.

591 ### 6.6.3 Manufacturing Profile Subcategories

592 ID.AM-3, PR.IP-1, DE.AE-1, DE-CM-7
593
594
595 ## 6.7 Change Control

596 Change control tools enable a manufacturer to document, track, and coordinate changes to
597 manufacturing system hardware and software components.

598 ### 6.7.1 Security Benefit

599 Changes often create unintended side effects that can cause outages or interruptions in operation.
600 Many outages can be prevented with effective configuration and change control programs.
601 Change control process ensures that changes are documented and appropriate personnel review
602 and approve of changes.
603
604 ### 6.7.2 Potential System Impacts

605 The creation, modification, and storage of change control documentation and procedures does
606 not have the ability to impact the manufacturing system.

607 ### 6.7.3 Manufacturing Profile Subcategories

608 PR.IP-1, PR.IP-3, PR.MA-1, DE.CM-7

609 **6.8 Configuration Backups**

610 Configuration backup tools enable a manufacturer to gather and archive configuration settings
611 from hardware and software components within the manufacturing system, typically in a data
612 format specified by the component OEM.

613 **6.8.1 Security Benefit**

614 Configuration backups allow the manufacturer to restore device configuration settings from
615 a known good state from a specific point in time. This is useful for quick recovery to an
616 operational state when incidents occur.
617
618 **6.8.2 Potential System Impacts**

619 Backup tools and methods used to obtain configuration backups can potentially impact the
620 manufacturing system as they could utilize excessive processing power or network bandwidth,
621 and sometimes require physical access to the device. Configuration backups should be planned
622 around scheduled downtime if possible.

623 **6.8.3 Manufacturing Profile Subcategories**

624 PR.IP-1, PR.IP-4
625
626
627 **6.9 Data Backup**

628 Data backup tools enable a manufacturer to collect and store files and programs from the
629 manufacturing system to facilitate recovery after an incident.

630 **6.9.1 Security Benefit**

631 Data backups allow data to be restored from an earlier point in time to help organizations recover
632 from incidents. These backups are an added layer of assurance in the case of a ransomware like
633 incident, ensuring critical data is backed up and stored offline. In addition, data recovered from
634 backups can also be leveraged for forensic investigations.

635 **6.9.2 Potential System Impacts**

636 Backup tools and methods used to obtain data backups can potentially impact the manufacturing
637 system as they could utilize excessive processing power or network bandwidth, and sometimes
638 require physical access to the device. Remote backups typically require a software agent to be
639 installed on the device. If possible, software agents should be configured to use the minimum
640 amount of processing power required for proper operation. Network-based data backups should
641 be configured to use the minimum amount of network bandwidth required for proper operation.
642 Data backups should be planned around scheduled downtime if possible.

643 **6.9.3 Manufacturing Profile Subcategories**

644 PR.IP-4
645

646 **6.10 Data Replication**

647 Data replication tools enable a manufacturer copy and transfer backup data to a physical location
648 external to the manufacturing system.

649 **6.10.1 Security Benefit**

650 Data Replication lets organizations stores their data in multiple locations, providing physical
651 separation and offline storage locations increases assurance to the data's integrity. This can be
652 accomplished via encryption tools that are used at both the hardware and software level thereby
653 providing guarantee to organizations that their data is safe from unauthorized access.

654 Replicating data to an offsite location makes your data disaster proof in the event of fire, flood or
655 other natural or man-made disasters

656 **6.10.2 Potential System Impacts**

657 The duplication of data and configuration backups should not impact the manufacturing system
658 as this operation is typically performed outside of the manufacturing system.

659 **6.10.3 Manufacturing Profile Subcategories**

660 PR.IP-4
661
662
663 **6.11 Network Segmentation and Segregation**

664 Network segmentation and segregation solutions enable a manufacturer to separate the
665 manufacturing system network from other networks (e.g., corporate networks, guest networks),
666 segment the internal manufacturing system network into smaller networks, and control the
667 communication between specific hosts and services.

668 **6.11.1 Security Benefit**

669 Network traffic can be isolated to limit access between different network segments and systems
670 hosting sensitive data can be isolated. Properly segmenting a network provides increased access
671 control, making it easier for IT administrators to restrict and monitor user access to systems. This
672 exercise also allows for improved performance because broadcast domain traffic is minimized as
673 number of systems are reduced on the same network segment, in turn reducing overall bandwidth
674 usage.

675 **6.11.2 Potential System Impacts**

676 Network segmentation and segregation can potentially impact the manufacturing system. Care
677 must be taken when planning and deploying network segmentation and segregation. Increased
678 network latency may occur, depending on the topology, hardware, and configuration of network
679 devices.

680 **6.11.3 Manufacturing Profile Subcategories**

681 PR.AC-5

682

683

684 **6.12 Network Boundary Protection**

685 Network boundary protection solutions enable a manufacturer to restrict data communication
686 traffic to and from manufacturing system network(s). Network boundary protection capabilities
687 include, but are not limited to, the use of firewalls, demilitarized zones (DMZ), and intrusion
688 detection and prevention systems.

689 **6.12.1 Security Benefit**

690 Firewalls allow organizations to segment their networks, restricting access to only allowed
691 connections. These devices monitor & log traffic accessing or attempting to access your network,
692 this functionality provides forensic data that can be critical for response and recovery activities.
693 More advanced firewalls, commonly called Next Generation Firewalls (NGFW), include
694 antivirus and malware protection with datasets continuously upgraded to detect new threats.
695 These NGFWs can provide other advanced security protections such as intrusion detection, deep
696 packet inspections, VPN services, and denial of service protection. The physical and logical
697 isolation characteristics of a DMZ are important because it enables access only to designated
698 servers and information stored within the isolated DMZ with no visibility directly into your
699 sensitive manufacturing network. Having a DMZ network reduces and controls access to those
700 internal systems from outside of the organization. Intrusion detection and prevention systems can
701 monitor, detect, analyze, and prevent unauthorized network or system access.

702 **6.12.2 Potential System Impacts**

703 Network boundary protections can potentially impact the manufacturing system. Care must be
704 taken when planning and deploying network boundary protections. Increased network latency
705 may be caused by in-line boundary protection devices (e.g., firewalls), especially if the
706 capabilities of the device and network do not match (e.g., a 100 Mbps Ethernet device on a 1
707 Gbps network).

708 **6.12.3 Manufacturing Profile Subcategories**

709 PR.AC-5, PR.PT-4, DE.CM-1

710

711

712 **6.13 Secure Remote Access**

713 Secure remote access solutions enable a manufacturer to establish secure communications
714 channels through which information can be transmitted over untrusted networks, including
715 public networks such as the Internet.

6.13.1 Security Benefit

Establishing these secure communications channels or encrypted tunnels allows a manufacturer to grant access to sensitive components in the manufacturing system for outside entities that can be used for activities including vendor upgrades, technical support, and remote employee access. When accessing the manufacturing system through a secure channel like a Virtual Private Network (VPN), data is encrypted and protected from a potential malicious actor.

More advanced implementations of this capability might use SSL based VPNs that perform security health checks on remote access devices, ensuring infected machines are not accessing critical system components.

6.13.2 Potential System Impacts

Secure remote access solutions can potentially impact the manufacturing system. Care must be taken if remote access is permitted while the manufacturing system is operational. Activities performed over a remote access connection may generate excessive network traffic. Remote access for maintenance activities should be planned around scheduled downtime.

6.13.3 Manufacturing Profile Subcategories

PR.AC-5, PR.MA-2, DE.CM-1

6.14 Managed Network Interfaces

Managed network interface solutions enable a manufacturer to control connections and information transmitted and received through individual physical ports on a network device.

6.14.1 Security Benefit

Managed network interfaces provide control over what is connected to a specific network and is critical to ensure unauthorized devices cannot be easily added to a network. When an unauthorized device is plugged into the network interface the managed interface will not send traffic until the port has been configured. Managed interfaces help ensure only identified devices can send traffic over a network.

6.14.2 Potential System Impacts

Managed network interface solutions can potentially impact the manufacturing system. Managed network interfaces can increase complexity during maintenance activities (e.g., upgrading network-based components, connecting maintenance computers to a local network).

6.14.3 Manufacturing Profile Subcategories

PR.AC-5

755 **6.15 Map Data Flows**

756 Data flow diagrams enable a manufacturer to understand the flow of data between networked
757 components of the manufacturing system.
758
759 **6.15.1 Security Benefit**

760 Documenting data flows enables organizations to understand expected behavior of their
761 networks. This understanding of how devices communicate assist with troubleshooting as well as
762 response and recovery activities. This information can be leveraged during forensic activities or
763 used for analysis to identify anomalies.
764
765 **6.15.2 Potential System Impacts**

766 Data flow mapping tools that use active scanning or require network monitoring tools, such as
767 network probes, can potentially impact the manufacturing system. Care must be taken before
768 using these tools to identify data flows on an operational system. Impacts could be due to the
769 nature of the information, the volume of network traffic, or momentary disconnection of
770 manufacturing system components from the network. Consider using data flow mapping tools
771 that utilize these methods during planned downtime.

772 **6.15.3 Manufacturing Profile Subcategories**

773 ID.AM-3, ID.AM-4, PR.AC-5, DE.AE-1
774
775
776 **6.16 Time Synchronization**

777 Time synchronization solutions enable a manufacturer to synchronize time for all manufacturing
778 system components to generate accurate timestamps.
779
780 **6.16.1 Security Benefit**

781 Time synchronization is critical for authentication protocols such as Kerberos in order to prevent
782 replay attacks. Time synchronization is also useful when correlating events or logs during
783 investigation purposes.
784
785 **6.16.2 Potential System Impacts**

786 Time synchronization should not impact the manufacturing system, but the effects of
787 unsynchronized time or misconfiguration can potentially impact services that require the time to
788 be synchronized.

789 **6.16.3 Manufacturing Profile Subcategories**

790 PR.PT-1
791

6.17 Credential Management

Credential management tools enables a manufacturer to manage the life cycle of user authentication credentials.

6.17.1 Security Benefit

Credential management enables manufactures to securely store and preform lifecycle management activities of credentials such as required password changes, defining privilege levels on a per user basis and the capability to revoke credentials. Some credentials management solutions minimize the attack surface by eliminating static and long-lived privilege grants.

6.17.2 Potential System Impacts

Credential management tools should not impact the manufacturing system, as they are not typically installed or operated within the manufacturing system.

6.17.3 Manufacturing Profile Subcategories

PR.AC-1, PR.MA-1, PR.MA-2

6.18 Authentication and Authorization

Authentication and authorization tools enable a manufacturer to verify the identity of a user, determine if a user has permission to access a system resource, and set the privileges each user has, including the principle of least privilege.

6.18.1 Security Benefit

With a centralized authentication system, users can access systems through a single set of login credentials. Consolidating authentication and authorization functionality on a single platform provides internal IT staff with a consistent method for managing user access. Least privilege ensures users/programs are given only permission required to perform their task.

6.18.2 Potential System Impacts

Authentication and authorization tools can potentially impact the manufacturing system. These tools typically require a software agent to be installed on the device. Backup authentication and authorization servers should be implemented to prevent operator "loss of view" and "loss of control" incidents. Manufacturers should determine where authentication and authorization is not advisable for performance, safety, or reliability reasons.

6.18.3 Manufacturing Profile Subcategories

PR.AC-1, PR.MA-1, PR.MA-2, PR-PT-3, PR.PT-4, DE.CM-3

6.19 Anti-virus/malware

Anti-virus/malware tools enable a manufacturer to monitor computing devices to identify all major types of malware and prevent or contain malware incidents.

6.19.1 Security Benefit

Malware is the most common threat for many manufactures. Anti-virus/malware tools can protect devices from being infected with malware, such as ransomware, viruses, worms, trojans, and malicious mobile code.

6.19.2 Potential System Impacts

Anti-virus/malware tools can potentially impact the manufacturing system. Anti-virus/malware may require a software agent to be installed on the device or may perform authenticated scanning via the network. If possible, these tools should be configured to use the minimum amount of processing power required for proper operation. Anti-virus/malware tools that utilize network-based authenticated scanning may generate excessive network traffic. These tools should be configured to use the minimum amount of network bandwidth required for proper operation. It is recommended that scans be planned around scheduled downtime.

6.19.3 Manufacturing Profile Subcategories

DE.CM-4

6.20 Risk Assessment

Risk assessment tools enable a manufacturer to perform risks assessments of the manufacturing system.

6.20.1 Security Benefit

A risk assessment will evaluate an organization's security posture by considering external as well as internal threats. In doing so, a risk assessment will identify current security vulnerabilities, control gaps, and noncompliance with standards. It is performed either via manual audits consisting of surveys, discussions, and/or questionnaires. Risk assessments are part of an overall risk management process, providing senior leaders/executives with the information needed to determine appropriate courses of action in response to identified risks. The results of these assessments can be leveraged to create awareness amongst employees and be used as a training tool as well. Performing regular risks assessments reduces incidents in the workplace.

6.20.2 Potential System Impacts

Risk assessment tools should not impact the manufacturing system, as they are typically operated and accessed outside of the manufacturing system.

6.20.3 Manufacturing Profile Subcategories

ID.RA-1

6.21 Vulnerability Scanning

Vulnerability scanning tools enable a manufacturer to scan, detect, and identify software flaws or misconfigurations that cause a weakness in the security of the manufacturing system.

6.21.1 Security Benefit

Identification of known security vulnerabilities present in the manufacturing network can be used to help inform patch management activities.

6.21.2 Potential System Impacts

Vulnerability scanning tools can impact an operational system. Vulnerability scanning tools may require a software agent to be installed on the device or may perform authenticated scanning via the network. Vulnerability scanning tools may generate excessive network traffic or, in extreme cases, cause device failures due to the intrusive methods used during scanning. These tools should be configured to use the minimum amount of network bandwidth required for proper operation. It is recommended that scans be planned around scheduled downtime and not be performed while the system is operational.

6.21.3 Manufacturing Profile Subcategories

ID.RA-1, DE.CM-8

6.22 Vulnerability Management

Vulnerability management tools enable a manufacturer to document, manage, and mitigate vulnerabilities discovered in the manufacturing system.

6.22.1 Security Benefit

Vulnerability management tools allows a manufacture to apply security updates to its systems and identify where compensating controls are needed to protect equipment that can't be updated.

6.22.2 Potential System Impacts

Vulnerability management can potentially impact the manufacturing system. A patch may remove a vulnerability, but it can also introduce a greater risk from a production or safety perspective. Patching a vulnerability may also change the way the operating system or application functions. It is recommended to consult with the product vendor to see if they have a list of approved patches and a vulnerability management process. It is recommended that vulnerability management be planned around scheduled downtime.

908 **6.22.3 Manufacturing Profile Subcategories**

909 ID.RA-1, DE.CM-4, RS.MI-3
910
911
912 **6.23 Incident Management**

913 Incident management tools enable a manufacturer to document, track, and coordinate the
914 mitigation of an adverse event in manufacturing system devices or networks.
915
916 **6.23.1 Security Benefit**

917 Incident management tools enable manufacturers to minimize downtimes due to incidents and
918 increase the efficiency and productivity of the manufacturing system. Information gained
919 during incident handling can be used to better prepare for handling any future incident.
920 Incident response plans enable organizations to act proactively before an incident or immediately
921 after an incident is noticed to limit the impact from incidents that occur.
922
923 **6.23.2 Potential System Impacts**

924 Incident management tools should not impact the manufacturing system, as they are typically
925 operated and accessed outside of the manufacturing system.

926 **6.23.3 Manufacturing Profile Subcategories**

927 RS.MI-2, RS.MI-3
928
929
930 **6.24 Network Monitoring**

931 Network monitoring tools enable a manufacturer to capture, store, and audit network traffic from
932 the manufacturing system networks, and monitor for indicators of potential cybersecurity
933 incidents.
934
935 **6.24.1 Security Benefit**

936 Network monitoring tools can identify suspicious traffic and other threat vectors, allowing
937 manufactures to respond fast to an incident. They can help to reduce incidents caused by human
938 error, configuration issues and other environmental factors. Effective network monitoring helps
939 to detect, diagnose, and resolve network performance issues, reducing incidents by proactively
940 identifying threats and bottlenecks.
941
942 **6.24.2 Potential System Impacts**

943 Network monitoring tools typically should not impact the manufacturing system, as they are
944 typically operated and accessed outside of the manufacturing system. However, certain methods
945 of capturing network traffic (e.g., network probes, mirror ports) can increase processing load on
946 network devices and can increase network latency.

947 **6.24.3 Manufacturing Profile Subcategories**

948 PR.DS-5, PR.MA-2, PR.PT-4, DE.CM-1, DE.CM-6, DE.CM-7
949
950
951 **6.25 System Use Monitoring**

952 System use monitoring solutions enable a manufacturer to monitor, store, audit, and restrict the
953 activities of manufacturing system users.
954
955 **6.25.1 Security Benefit**

956 Monitoring systems and users within the organizations manufacturing environment helps to
957 ensure users and systems are behaving as expected. This capability can also aid in
958 troubleshooting when an issue occurs by providing information about which users where
959 working within the system during the time period. Monitoring also helps show if there is a
960 misconfiguration introduced in the manufacturing system.
961
962 **6.25.2 Potential System Impacts**

963 System use monitoring tools can potentially impact the manufacturing system. These tools
964 typically require a software agent to be installed on the device, utilizing processing power and
965 network bandwidth. If possible, software agents should be configured to use the minimum
966 amount of processing power required for proper operation.

967 **6.25.3 Manufacturing Profile Subcategories**

968 PR.AC-1, PR.DS-3, PR.MA-2, DE.CM-3
969
970
971 **6.26 Maintenance Tracking**

972 Maintenance tracking solutions enable a manufacturer to schedule, track, authorize, monitor, and
973 audit maintenance and repair activities to manufacturing system computing devices.
974
975 **6.26.1 Security Benefit**

976 Tracking changes to devices within the manufacturing system ensures visibility into maintenance
977 logs and changes performed. Tracking these events also provides an audit trail that can aid in
978 troubleshooting, response, and recovery activities. Maintenance tracking can also provide
979 visibility into when components should be serviced and help inform end of life decisions. This
980 type of tracking also helps changes to be coordinated in advance as to not cause disruption within
981 manufacturing system.
982
983 **6.26.2 Potential System Impacts**

984 Maintenance tracking tools should not impact the manufacturing system, as they are typically
985 operated and accessed outside of the manufacturing system.

986 ### 6.26.3 Manufacturing Profile Subcategories

987 PR.MA-1, PR.MA-2
988
989
990 ## 6.27 Physical Access Control

991 Physical access control solutions enable a manufacturer to deny or restrict access to the
992 manufacturing system by unauthorized individuals.
993
994 ### 6.27.1 Security Benefit

995 Limiting physical access to only authorized individuals protects manufacturing system from
996 malicious actors getting local access to critical components. These protections also help prevent
997 accidental or unintentional damage.
998
999 ### 6.27.2 Potential System Impacts

1000 Physical access control tools should not impact the manufacturing system.

1001 ### 6.27.3 Manufacturing Profile Subcategories

1002 PR.AC-2, PR.DS-5, PR.MA-1
1003

1004 ## 6.28 Physical Access Monitoring

1005 Physical access monitoring solutions enable a manufacturer to record, monitor, archive, and
1006 audit physical access to the manufacturing system by all individuals.
1007
1008 ### 6.28.1 Security Benefit

1009 The ability to record, monitor, archive and audit physical access to the manufacturing facility and
1010 locations within allows provides visibility into physical presence during activities being
1011 performed. These logs can be correlated with logical logs to help identify malicious threat actors
1012 and other harmful activity.
1013
1014 ### 6.28.2 Potential System Impacts

1015 Physical access monitoring tools should not impact the manufacturing system.

1016 ### 6.28.3 Manufacturing Profile Subcategories

1017 PR.AC-2, PR.PT-1, DE.CM-2, DE.CM-3
1018
1019
1020

6.29 Ports and Services Lockdown

Ports and services lockdown solutions enable a manufacturer to discover and disable nonessential physical and logical network ports and services.

6.29.1 Security Benefit

The ability to discover and disable unused physical ports within the manufacturing will prevent rogue devices from being able to connect to the network. These types of devices could create a potential entry point for malicious threat actors. A comprehensive understanding of which logical ports are in use and the services are required within the network provides additional defense in depth protection.

6.29.2 Potential System Impacts

Locking-down ports and services can potentially impact the manufacturing system. Care must be taken to understand the role of all ports and services before they are disabled to verify they are not required for manufacturing system operations.

6.29.3 Manufacturing Profile Subcategories

PR.IP-1, PR.PT-3

6.30 Media Protection

Media protection solutions enable a manufacturer to restrict the use of portable media within the manufacturing system.

6.30.1 Security Benefit

Media protection solutions reduce the threat of unknown and potentially malicious devices being connected to the manufacturing system equipment.

6.30.2 Potential System Impacts

Media protection solutions can potentially impact the manufacturing system. Media protection for privileged users may be impactful to the manufacturing system by limiting their ability to respond to a manufacturing system event or incident. Care must be taken to verify privileged users have the access required to perform their roles and functions.

6.30.3 Manufacturing Profile Subcategories

PR.PT-2

6.31 Encryption

Encryption solutions enable a manufacturer to encode sensitive manufacturing system data so that only authorized users can access it.

6.31.1 Security Benefit

Encryption provides data confidentiality when data is in use, in transit or at rest by converting plaintext into ciphertext that can only be viewed by recipients having the correct keys. If data is compromised or leaked the likelihood of sensitive information being exposed would be minimized.

6.31.2 Potential System Impacts

Tools that perform methods of encryption can potentially impact the manufacturing system. Computational operations to encrypt and decrypt data require processing power and memory. These effects can be exacerbated when they are executed on embedded devices. Depending on the encryption and decryption methods used, time-sensitive data communications may also be impacted. Physical network devices used to encrypt traffic between multiple devices may increase network latency.

6.31.3 Manufacturing Profile Subcategories

PR.DS-5

6.32 Data Loss Prevention

Data loss prevention solutions enable a manufacturer to detect and prevent the unauthorized use and transmission of sensitive manufacturing system data.

6.32.1 Security Benefit

Detect and prevents exposure of sensitive information across network devices.

6.32.2 Potential System Impacts

Network-based data loss prevention tools that monitor and detect for data loss should not typically impact the manufacturing system. Data loss prevention tools that are implemented as in-line network devices can potentially increase network latency across the boundary potentially block all network traffic during a power or software failure. Endpoint-based data loss prevention tools can potentially impact the manufacturing system, as they utilize processing power and/or network bandwidth. If possible, these tools should be configured to use the minimum amount of processing power required for proper operation.

6.32.3 Manufacturing Profile Subcategories

PR.DS-5

1098 **6.33 Media Sanitization**

1099 Media sanitization solutions enable a manufacturer to render data written on media
1100 unrecoverable.
1101
1102 **6.33.1 Security Benefit**

1103 Media sanitization solutions ensure confidential information is removed/destroyed from any
1104 device containing storage media, such as USB drives, external hard drives and internal hard
1105 drives. Devices not sanitized appropriately can become a security concern when decommissioned
1106 items are no longer in the company's possession.
1107
1108 **6.33.2 Potential System Impacts**

1109 Media sanitization tools should not impact the manufacturing system, as they are typically
1110 operated outside of the manufacturing system.

1111 **6.33.3 Manufacturing Profile Subcategories**

1112 PR.DS-3, PR-IP-6
1113
1114
1115 **6.34 Event Logging**

1116 Event logging solutions enable a manufacturer to capture, store, archive, and audit the events
1117 occurring within the manufacturing system and its networks.
1118
1119 **6.34.1 Security Benefit**

1120 Event logging provides important information with regard to operations of the system. This
1121 information can aid in improving reporting, log collection, analysis and can help preventing
1122 potential security breaches. Robust logging capabilities help meet any compliance requirements
1123 as well as reducing the impact of security incidents.
1124
1125 **6.34.2 Potential System Impacts**

1126 Event logging solutions can potentially impact the manufacturing system. In order for the event
1127 logger to operate properly, devices within the manufacturing system must generate messages
1128 destined for the logger. Network bandwidth will be consumed to send these messages, and the
1129 amount of traffic is highly dependent on the number of hosts and the configured logging level
1130 (e.g., critical errors, warnings, debug). A balance must be found between the amount of
1131 consumed network bandwidth and the desired logging level. Processing load may increase on
1132 devices that send large number of messages to the event logger.

1133 **6.34.3 Manufacturing Profile Subcategories**

1134 PR.PT-1, DE.AE-3, DE.CM-1, DE.CM-6, DE.DP-3, RS.AN-3
1135
1136

1137 **6.35 Forensics**

1138 Forensic solutions enable a manufacturer to identify, collect, examine, and analyze data from the
1139 manufacturing system to determine the cause of an incident.
1140
1141 **6.35.1 Security Benefit**

1142 Collection of forensics related data within a network environment provides the ability to examine
1143 network data for additional evidence needed to determine malicious activities and identify
1144 potential actors. Collections of system/network logs can help identify threat actors for
1145 prosecution. Forensics logs are also useful if the situation requires help from an outside incident
1146 response company.
1147
1148 **6.35.2 Potential System Impacts**

1149 Forensic tools should not impact the manufacturing system, as they are typically operated outside
1150 of the manufacturing system.

1151 **6.35.3 Manufacturing Profile Subcategories**

1152 DE.AE-2
1153

1154

Function	Category	Subcategory	Hardware Inventory	Software Inventory	Systems Development Lifecycle Management	Network Architecture Documentation	Configuration Management	Baseline Establishment	Change Control	Configuration Backups	Data Backup	Data Replication	Network Segmentation and Segregation	Network Boundary Protection	Secure Remote Access	Managed Network Interfaces	Map Data Flows	Time Synchronization	Credential Management	Authentication and Authorization	Anti-virus/malware	Risk Assessment	Vulnerability Scanning	Vulnerability Management	Incident Management	Network Monitoring	System Use Monitoring	Maintenance Tracking	Physical Access Control	Physical Access Monitoring	Ports and Services Lockdown	Media Protection	Encryption	Data Loss Prevention	Media Sanitization	Event Logging	Forensics
ID	Asset Management	ID.AM-1	•																																		
ID	Asset Management	ID.AM-2		•																																	
ID	Asset Management	ID.AM-3				•	•	•									•																				
ID	Asset Management	ID.AM-4				•	•										•																				
ID	Risk Assessment	ID.RA-1																				•	•	•													
PR	Access Control	PR.AC-1																	•	•							•										
PR	Access Control	PR.AC-2																											•	•							
PR	Access Control	PR.AC-5											•	•	•	•	•	•																			
PR	Data Security	PR.DS-3	•	•	•																														•		
PR	Data Security	PR.DS-5																								•	•		•				•	•			
PR	Information Protection Processes and Procedures	PR.IP-1			•		•	•	•	•																					•						
PR	Information Protection Processes and Procedures	PR.IP-2			•																																
PR	Information Protection Processes and Procedures	PR.IP-3							•																												
PR	Information Protection Processes and Procedures	PR.IP-4					•			•	•	•																									
PR	Information Protection Processes and Procedures	PR.IP-6			•																														•		
PR	Maintenance	PR.MA-1					•		•										•	•									•	•							
PR	Maintenance	PR.MA-2													•				•	•						•	•	•									
PR	Protective Technology	PR.PT-1																•												•						•	
PR	Protective Technology	PR.PT-2																														•					
PR	Protective Technology	PR.PT-3																						•							•						
PR	Protective Technology	PR.PT-4											•											•		•											
DE	Anomalies and Events	DE.AE-1						•											•																		
DE	Anomalies and Events	DE.AE-2																																			•
DE	Anomalies and Events	DE.AE-3																																		•	
DE	Security Continuous Monitoring	DE.CM-1											•													•										•	
DE	Security Continuous Monitoring	DE.CM-2																												•							
DE	Security Continuous Monitoring	DE.CM-3																			•						•		•								
DE	Security Continuous Monitoring	DE.CM-4																				•			•												
DE	Security Continuous Monitoring	DE.CM-6																								•										•	
DE	Security Continuous Monitoring	DE.CM-7	•	•	•			•	•																	•											
DE	Security Continuous Monitoring	DE.CM-8																					•														
DE	Detection Processes	DE.DP-3																																		•	
RS	Analysis	RS.AN-3																																		•	•
RS	Mitigation	RS.MI-2																							•												
RS	Mitigation	RS.MI-3																						•	•												

1155
1156   Table 6-1. Mapping of CSF Manufacturing Profile Subcategories to Technical Capabilities
1157

1158   Table 6-1 summarizes the information discussed in this Section and shows the coverage of CSF
1159   Manufacturing Profile Subcategories addressed when the technical capabilities are implemented
1160   as part of a cybersecurity program.

7. Capabilities Mapping to Manufacturing Profile

This section examines the policies and procedures, described in Section 5, and/or technical solutions, described in Section 6, required to meet the language specified in each particular Subcategory, and lists potential solutions that fulfil the requirements that are accessible by small manufactures. Accessibility criteria included cost, ease of use, and level of effort to implement. The list of potential solutions is not intended to be all inclusive, but to provide examples. Specific solutions that were implemented in the lab environment for each use case are included in Volume 2 and Volume 3.

Function	Category	Subcategory	Manufacturing Profile	Implementation Overview
			Low	
IDENTIFY	Asset Management (ID.AM)	ID.AM-1	Document an inventory of manufacturing system components that reflects the current system. Manufacturing system components include for example PLCs, sensors, actuators, robots, machine tools, firmware, network switches, routers, power supplies, and other networked components or devices. System component inventory is reviewed and updated as defined by the organization. Information deemed necessary for effective accountability of manufacturing system components includes, for example, hardware inventory specifications, component owners, networked components or devices, machine names and network addresses. Inventory specifications include, for example, manufacturer, device type, model, serial number, and physical location.	These subcategory requirements can be met by implementing solutions that provide the **Hardware Inventory** technical capability. Potential solutions for meeting these subcategory requirements include: Open-AudIT, Nmap, LANSweeper, Spiceworks, OCSinventory-ng, Excel (manual entry) Solutions that were implemented in use cases: Open-AudIT
			Low	
		ID.AM-2	Document an inventory of manufacturing system software components that reflects the current system. Manufacturing system software components include for example software license information, software version numbers, HMI and other ICS component applications, software, operating systems. System software inventory is reviewed and updated as defined by the organization.	These subcategory requirements can be met by implementing solutions that provide the **Software Inventory** technical capability. Potential solutions for meeting these subcategory requirements include: Open-AudIT, Nmap, LANSweeper, Spiceworks, OCSinventory-ng, Excel (manual entry) Solutions that were implemented in use cases: Open-AudIT

Function	Category	Subcategory	Manufacturing Profile	Implementation Overview
IDENTIFY	**Asset Management (ID.AM)**	**ID.AM-3**	**Low** Document all connections within the manufacturing system, and between the manufacturing system and other systems. All connections are documented, authorized, and reviewed. Connection information includes, for example, the interface characteristics, data characteristics, ports, protocols, addresses, description of the data, security requirements, and the nature of the connection.	These subcategory requirements can be met by implementing solutions that provide the **Network Architecture Documentation, Configuration Management, Baseline Establishment, and Map Data Flows** technical capabilities. Potential solutions for meeting these subcategory requirements include: GRASSMARLIN, Microsoft Visio, Wireshark, Nmap, Open-AudIT, Tenable Nessus, Ntopng Solutions that were implemented in use cases GRASSMARLIN Microsoft Visio Wireshark Open-AudIT
		ID.AM-4	**Low** Identify and document all external connections for the manufacturing system. Examples of external systems include engineering design services, and those that are controlled under separate authority, personal devices, and other hosted services.	These subcategory requirements can be met by implementing solutions that provide the **Network Architecture Documentation, Configuration Management, and Map Data Flows** technical capabilities. Potential solutions for meeting these subcategory requirements include: GRASSMARLIN, Microsoft Visio, Wireshark, Nmap, Open-AudIT, Tenable Nessus, Ntopng Solutions that were implemented in use cases GRASSMARLIN Microsoft Visio Wireshark Open-AudIT

Function	Category	Subcategory	Manufacturing Profile	Implementation Overview
IDENTIFY	Asset Management (ID.AM)	ID.AM-5	**Low** Identify and prioritize manufacturing system components and functions based on their classification, criticality, and business value. Identify the types of information in possession, custody, or control for which security safeguards are needed (e.g. sensitive or protected information).	These subcategory requirements can be met by developing policies and procedures in the **Asset Criticality Matrix** section of the **Risk Management** document
		ID.AM-6	**Low** Establish and maintain personnel cybersecurity roles and responsibilities for the manufacturing system. Include cybersecurity roles and responsibilities for third-party providers. Third-party providers are required to notify the organization of any personnel transition (including transfers or terminations) involving personnel with physical or logical access to the manufacturing system components. Third-party providers include, for example, service providers, contractors, and other organizations providing manufacturing system development, technology services, outsourced applications, or network and security management.	These subcategory requirements can be met by developing policies and procedures in the **Role-based Security Responsibilities** section of the **Security Policy** document
	Business Environment (ID.BE)	ID.BE-1	**Low** Define and communicate the organization's role in the supply chain. Identify the upstream and downstream supply channels that are outside of the organization's operations. Identify the overall mission supported by the manufacturing system.	These subcategory requirements can be met by developing policies and procedures in the **Organization Overview** section of the **Security Program** document.
		ID.BE-2	**Low** Define and communicate the manufacturer's place in critical infrastructure and its industry sector. Define and communicate critical infrastructure and key resources relevant to the manufacturing system. Develop, document, and maintain a critical infrastructure and key resources protection plan.	These subcategory requirements can be met by developing policies and procedures in the **Organization Overview** section of the **Security Program** document.

Function	Category	Subcategory	Manufacturing Profile	Implementation Overview
IDENTIFY		ID.BE-3	**Low** Establish and communicate priorities for manufacturing missions, objectives, and activities with consideration for security and the resulting risk to manufacturing operations, components, and individuals. Identify critical manufacturing system components and functions by performing a criticality analysis.	These subcategory requirements can be met by developing policies and procedures in the **Organization Overview** section of the **Security Program** document.
	Business Environment (ID.BE)	ID.BE-4	**Low** Identify and prioritize supporting services for critical manufacturing system processes and components. Provide an uninterruptable power supply for identified critical manufacturing system components to facilitate the transition of the manufacturing system to long-term alternate power in the event of a primary power source loss.	These subcategory requirements can be met by developing policies and procedures in the **Organization Overview** and **Emergency Power** sections of the **Security Program** document.
		ID.BE-5	**Low** Establish resilience requirements for the manufacturing system to support delivery of critical services.	These subcategory requirements can be met by developing policies and procedures in the **RPO and RTO Targets** section of the **Incident Recovery** document
	Governance (ID.GV)	ID.GV-1	**Low** Develop and disseminate a security policy that provides an overview of the security requirements for the manufacturing system. The policy includes, for example, the identification and assignment of roles, responsibilities, management commitment, coordination among organizational entities, and compliance. It also reflects coordination among organizational entities responsible for the different aspects of security (i.e., technical, physical, personnel, cyber-physical, access control, media protection, vulnerability management, maintenance, monitoring), and covers the full life cycle of the manufacturing system. Review and update the security policy as determined necessary. Ensure the security policy is approved by a senior official with responsibility and accountability for the risk being incurred by manufacturing operations.	These subcategory requirements can be met by developing policies and procedures in the **Security Policy** document

Function	Category	Subcategory	Manufacturing Profile	Implementation Overview
IDENTIFY		**ID.GV-2**	**Low** Develop and disseminate a security program for the manufacturing system that includes, for example, the identification of personnel security roles and assignment of responsibilities, management commitment, coordination among organizational entities, and compliance. This includes security requirements, roles and responsibilities for third-party providers. Review and update the security program as determined necessary.	These subcategory requirements can be met by developing policies and procedures in the **Security Program** document
		ID.GV-3	**Low** Ensure that legal and regulatory requirements affecting the manufacturing operations regarding cybersecurity are understood and managed.	These subcategory requirements can be met by developing policies and procedures in the **Applicable Laws and Regulations** section of the **Security Program** document.
	Governance (ID.GV)	**ID.GV-4**	**Low** Develop a comprehensive strategy to manage risk to manufacturing operations. Include cybersecurity considerations in the risk management strategy. Review and update the risk management strategy as determined necessary. Determine and allocate required resources to protect the manufacturing system.	These subcategory requirements can be met by developing policies and procedures in the **Risk Management** document

Function	Category	Subcategory	Manufacturing Profile	Implementation Overview
IDENTIFY	**Risk Assessment (ID.RA)**	**ID.RA-1**	**Low** Develop a plan to identify, document, and report vulnerabilities that exist on the manufacturing system. Include the use of vulnerability scanning where safe and feasible on the manufacturing system, its components, or a representative system.	Some of these subcategory requirements can be met by implementing solutions that provide the **Risk Assessment, Vulnerability Scanning and Vulnerability Management** technical capabilities. Potential solutions for meeting these subcategory requirements include: DHS Cybersecurity Evaluation Tool (CSET), NamicSoft, OpenVAS, Tenable Nessus, AlienVault OSSIM, Microsoft Excel (Manual) Solutions that were implemented in use cases: CSET NamicSoft Tenable Nessus Some of these subcategory requirements can be met by developing policies and procedures in the **Vulnerability Management Process** section of the **Procedures** document
		ID.RA-2	**Low** Establish and maintain ongoing contact with security groups and associations, and receive security alerts and advisories. Security groups and associations include, for example, special interest groups, forums, professional associations, news groups, and/or peer groups of security professionals in similar organizations. Implement a threat awareness program that includes a cross-organization information-sharing capability. Organizations should consider having both an unclassified and classified information sharing capability. Collaborate and share information about potential vulnerabilities and incidents on a timely basis. The DHS National Cybersecurity & Communications Integration Center (NCCIC) [6] serves as a centralized location where operational elements involved in cybersecurity and communications reliance are coordinated and integrated. The Industrial Control Systems Cyber Emergency Response Team (ICS-CERT) [7] collaborates with international and private sector Computer Emergency Response Teams (CERTs) to share control systems-related security incidents and mitigation measures.	These subcategory requirements can be met by developing policies and procedures in the **Information Sharing Plan** and **Security Awareness Training** sections of **Security Program** document, **Risk Identification** section of **Risk Management** document, and **Guidelines for Information Sharing** section of **Incident Response Plan** document.

Function	Category	Subcategory	Manufacturing Profile	Implementation Overview
IDENTIFY	Risk Assessment (ID.RA)	ID.RA-3	**Low** Conduct and document periodic assessment of risk to the manufacturing system that takes into account threats and likelihood of impact to manufacturing operations and assets. The risk assessment includes threats from insiders and external parties.	These subcategory requirements can be met by developing policies and procedures in the **Risk, Monitor and Control** section of the **Risk Management** document
		ID.RA-4	**Low** Conduct criticality reviews of the manufacturing system that define the potential adverse impacts to manufacturing operations, assets, and individuals if compromised or disabled.	These subcategory requirements can be met by developing policies and procedures in the **Periodic Reviews** section of the **Risk Management** document
		ID.RA-5	**Low** Conduct risk assessments of the manufacturing system incorporating threats, vulnerabilities, likelihood, and impact to manufacturing operations, assets, and individuals. Disseminate risk assessment results to relevant stakeholders.	These subcategory requirements can be met by developing policies and procedures in the **Risk Monitor and Control** and **Risk Reporting** sections of the **Risk Management** document
		ID.RA-6	**Low** Develop and implement a comprehensive strategy to manage risk to the manufacturing system that includes the identification and prioritization of risk responses.	These subcategory requirements can be met by developing policies and procedures in the **Risk Management** document
	Risk Management Strategy (ID.RM)	ID.RM-1	**Low** Establish a risk management process for the manufacturing system that effectively identifies, communicates, and facilitates addressing risk-related issues and information among key stakeholders internally and externally.	These subcategory requirements can be met by developing policies and procedures in the **Risk Notification Process** section of the **Risk Management** document
		ID.RM-2	**Low** Define the risk tolerance for the manufacturing system.	These subcategory requirements can be met by developing policies and procedures in the **Risk Tolerance** section of the **Risk Management** document
		ID.RM-3	**Low** Ensure the risk tolerance for the manufacturing system is informed by the organization's role in critical infrastructure and sector-specific risk analysis.	These subcategory requirements can be met by developing policies and procedures in the **Risk Tolerance** section of the **Risk Management** document

Function	Category	Subcategory	Manufacturing Profile	Implementation Overview
PROTECT	Access Control (PR.AC)	PR.AC-1	**Low** Establish and manage identification mechanisms and credentials for users and of the manufacturing system.	These subcategory requirements can be met by implementing solutions that provide the **Credential Management, Authentication and Authorization, and System Use Monitoring** technical capabilities. Potential solutions for meeting these subcategory requirements include: Microsoft Active Directory, FreeIPA, OpenLDAP, native operating system/device capabilities Solutions that were implemented in use cases: Microsoft Active Directory Native operating system/device capabilities
		PR.AC-2	**Low** Protect physical access to the manufacturing facility. Determine access requirements during emergency situations. Maintain and review visitor access records to the facility where the manufacturing system resides. Physical access controls may include, for example, lists of authorized individuals, identity credentials, escort requirements, guards, fences, turnstiles, locks, monitoring of facility access.	These subcategory requirements can be met by implementing solutions that provide the **Physical Access Control and Physical Access Monitoring** technical capabilities. Potential solutions for meeting these subcategory requirements include: lists of authorized individuals, sign in/out sheets, identity credentials, escort requirements, guards, fences, turnstiles, locks, electronic access control systems, cameras, monitoring of facility access. Solutions that were implemented in use cases: Locks Fences Electronic Access Control System Sign in/out sheet
		PR.AC-3	**Low** Establish usage restrictions, connection requirements, implementation guidance, and authorizations for remote access to the manufacturing system. Provide an explicit indication of active remote access connections to users physically present at the devices. Remote access methods include, for example, wireless, dial-up, broadband, VPN connections, mobile device connections, and communications through external networks.	These subcategory requirements can be met by developing policies and procedures in the **Remote Access** section of the **Security Policy** document

Function	Category	Subcategory	Manufacturing Profile	Implementation Overview
PROTECT	Access Control (PR.AC)	PR.AC-4	**Low** Define and manage access permissions for users of the manufacturing system. Identify and document user actions that can be performed on the manufacturing system without identification or authentication (e.g. during emergencies).	These subcategory requirements can be met by developing policies and procedures in the **Actions with/without Authentication** section of the **Standard Operating Procedures** document
		PR.AC-5	**Low** Protect network integrity of the manufacturing system, incorporating network segmentation and segregation where appropriate. Identify and control connections between system components. Monitor and control connections and communications at the external boundary and at key internal boundaries within the manufacturing system. Employ boundary protection devices. Boundary protection mechanisms include, for example, routers, gateways, unidirectional gateways, data diodes, and firewalls separating system components into logically separate networks or subnetworks.	These subcategory requirements can be met by implementing solutions that provide the **Network Segmentation and Segregation, Network Boundary Protection, Secure Remote Access, Managed Network Interfaces, Map Data Flows** technical capabilities. Potential solutions for meeting these subcategory requirements include: routers, gateways, unidirectional gateways, data diodes, firewalls, DMZ, switches, SNORT, BRO, VPNs, remote desktops, Native operating system/device capabilities, GRASSMARLIN, Microsoft Visio, Wireshark, Ntopng Solutions that were implemented in use cases: Routers Firewalls DMZ Switches VPNs TeamViewer Native operating system/device capabilities GRASSMARLIN Microsoft Visio Wireshark
	Awareness and Training (PR.AT)	PR.AT-1	**Low** Provide security awareness training for all manufacturing system users and managers. Training could include, for example, a basic understanding of the protections and user actions needed to maintain security of the system, responding to suspected cybersecurity incidents, and awareness of operational security.	These subcategory requirements can be met by developing policies and procedures in the **Security Awareness Training** section of the **Security Program** document

CSF Mfg Profile Low Sec Lvl Example IG General Implementation Guidance

Function	Category	Subcategory	Manufacturing Profile	Implementation Overview
PROTECT		PR.AT-2	**Low** Ensure that users with privileged access to the manufacturing system understand the requirements and responsibilities of their assignments. Establish standards for measuring, building, and validating individual qualifications for privileged users.	These subcategory requirements can be met by developing policies and procedures in the **Security Awareness Training** section of the **Security Program** document
	Awareness and Training (PR.AT)	PR.AT-3	**Low** Establish and enforce security requirements for third-party providers and users. Ensure that third-party providers understand their responsibilities regarding the security of the manufacturing system and the responsibilities of their assignments. Require notifications be given for any personnel transfers, termination, or transition involving personnel with physical or logical access to the manufacturing system components. Ensure that providers of external system services comply with defined security requirements. Monitor and audit external service providers for security compliance.	These subcategory requirements can be met by developing policies and procedures in the **Security Awareness Training and Third party responsibilities and requirements** section of the **Security Program** document.
		PR.AT-4	**Low** Ensure that senior executives understand the requirements for the security and protection of the manufacturing system, and their responsibilities for achieving them.	These subcategory requirements can be met by developing policies and procedures in the **Commitment from Management** section of the **Security Program** document
		PR.AT-5	**Low** Ensure that personnel responsible for the physical protection and security of the manufacturing system and facility are trained for, and understand their responsibilities. Establish standards for measuring, building, and validating individual qualifications for physical security personnel.	These subcategory requirements can be met by developing policies and procedures in the **Employee Requirements** section of the **Security Policy** document
	Data Security (PR.DS)	PR.DS-1	**Low** None	N/A
		PR.DS-2	**Low** None	N/A

Function	Category	Subcategory	Manufacturing Profile	Implementation Overview
			Low	
PROTECT		PR.DS-3	Enforce accountability for all manufacturing system components throughout the system lifecycle, including removal, transfers, and disposition. Sanitize portable media prior to disposal, release, or reuse. All system components entering and exiting the facility are authorized, monitored, and controlled, and records are maintained of those items.	Some of these subcategory requirements can be met by implementing solutions that provide the **Hardware Inventory, Software Inventory, Systems Development Lifecycle Management, and Media Sanitization** technical capabilities. Potential solutions for meeting these subcategory requirements include: Open-AudIT, LANSweeper, Spiceworks, OCSinventory-ng, AlienVault OSSIM, MS Excel (Manual), media sanitization tools. Solutions that were implemented in use cases: Open-AudIT DBAN Some of these subcategory requirements can be met by developing policies and procedures in the **Lifecycle Accountability of Devices** section of the **Security Policy** document and **Media Sanitization Procedures** of the **Standard Operating Procedures** document.
	Data Security (PR.DS)		**Low**	
		PR.DS-4	Ensure that adequate resources are maintained for manufacturing system information processing, networking, telecommunications, and data storage. Off-load audit records from the manufacturing system for processing to an alternate system.	These subcategory requirements can be met by developing policies and procedures in the **Event Logging** and **Ensure Resources are Maintained** sections of the **Standard Operating Procedures** document.

Function	Category	Subcategory	Manufacturing Profile	Implementation Overview
PROTECT	Data Security (PR.DS)	PR.DS-5	**Low** Protect the manufacturing system against data leaks. Monitor the manufacturing system at the external boundary and at key internal points to detect unauthorized access and use. Develop and document access agreements for all users of the manufacturing system.	Some of these subcategory requirements can be met by implementing solutions that provide the **Network Monitoring, System Use Monitoring, Physical Access Control, Encryption, and Data Loss Prevention** technical capabilities. Potential solutions for meeting these subcategory requirements include: Security Onion, SNORT, Suricata, Zeek Network Security Monitor, Native operating system/device capabilities, lists of authorized individuals, sign in/out sheets, identity credentials, escort requirements, guards, fences, turnstiles, locks, electronic access control systems, cameras, monitoring of facility access, Microsoft EFS, Microsoft BitLocker, AxCrypt, VeraCrypt, GTB Inspector, Comodo DOME Solutions that were implemented in use cases: Security Onion Microsoft EFS Locks Fences Electronic Access Control System Sign in/out sheets GTB Inspector VeraCrypt
		PR.DS-6	**Low** None	Some of these subcategory requirements can be met by developing policies and procedures in the **User Access Agreement** section of the **Security Policy** document N/A
		PR.DS-7	**Low** None	N/A

Function	Category	Subcategory	Manufacturing Profile	Implementation Overview
PROTECT	Information Protection Processes and Procedures (PR.IP)	PR.IP-1	**Low** Develop, document, and maintain a baseline configuration for the manufacturing system. Baseline configurations include for example, information about manufacturing system components, software version information, software license information, current version numbers and patch information on operating systems and applications; and configuration settings/parameters), network topology, and the logical placement of those components within the system architecture. Configure the manufacturing system to provide only essential capabilities. Review the baseline configuration and disable unnecessary capabilities.	These subcategory requirements can be met by implementing solutions that provide the **Systems Development Lifecycle Management, Configuration Management, Baseline Establishment, Change Control, Configuration Backups, and Ports and Services Lockdown** technical capabilities. Potential solutions for meeting these subcategory requirements include: Open-AudIT, LANSweeper, Spiceworks, OCSinventory-ng, Microsoft Excel (Manual), I-doit, Salt, Puppet, Ansible, GRASSMARLIN, Wireshark, Nmap and Native operating system/device capabilities Solutions that were implemented in use cases: Open-AudIT Microsoft Excel GRASSMARLIN Wireshark Native operating system/device capabilities
		PR.IP-2	**Low** Manage the manufacturing system using a system development life cycle that includes security considerations. Include security requirements into the acquisition process of the manufacturing system and its components.	These subcategory requirements can be met by implementing solutions that provide the **Systems Development Lifecycle Management** technical capability. Potential solutions for meeting these subcategory requirements include: Open-AudIT, LANSweeper, Spiceworks, OCSinventory-ng, MS Excel (Manual) Solutions that were implemented in use cases: Open-AudIT

Function	Category	Subcategory	Manufacturing Profile	Implementation Overview
			Low	
		PR.IP-3	Employ configuration change control for the manufacturing system and its components. Conduct security impact analyses in connection with change control reviews.	Some of these subcategory requirements can be met by implementing solutions that provide the **Change Control** technical capability. Potential solutions for meeting these subcategory requirements include: Open-AudIT, GRASSMARLIN, Wireshark, I-doit, Salt, Puppet, Ansible. Solutions that were implemented in use cases: Open-AudIT GRASSMARLIN Wireshark Some of these subcategory requirements can be met by developing policies and Procedures in the **Change Control** section of the **Operating Procedures** document.
PROTECT	Information Protection Processes and Procedures (PR.IP)		**Low**	
		PR.IP-4	Conduct and maintain backups for manufacturing system data. Manufacturing system data includes for example software, configurations and settings, documentation, system configuration data including computer configuration backups, application configuration backups, operational control limits, control bands and set points for pre-incident operation for all ICS programmable equipment	These subcategory requirements can be met by implementing solutions that provide the **Configuration Management, Change Control, Configuration Backups, Data Backup, and Data Replication** technical capabilities. Potential solutions for meeting these subcategory requirements include: Open-AudIT, I-doit, Salt, Puppet, Ansible, Veeam Backup and Replication, Bacula Systems, Clonezilla, Commvault Backup & Recovery, Redo backup, and Native operating system/device capabilities. Solutions that were implemented in use cases: Open-AudIT Veeam Backup and Replication Native operating system/device capabilities.

Function	Category	Subcategory	Manufacturing Profile	Implementation Overview
PROTECT	Information Protection Processes and Procedures (PR.IP)	PR.IP-5	**Low** Define, implement, and enforce policy and regulations regarding emergency and safety systems, fire protection systems, and environment controls for the manufacturing system. Fire suppression mechanisms should take the manufacturing environment into account (e.g., water sprinkler systems could be hazardous in specific environments).	These subcategory requirements can be met by developing policies and procedures in the **Fire and Safety Regulations** section of the **Security Program** document.
		PR.IP-6	**Low** Ensure that manufacturing system data is destroyed according to policy. Apply nondestructive sanitization techniques to portable storage devices connecting to the manufacturing system.	These subcategory requirements can be met by implementing solutions that provide the **Systems Development Lifecycle Management and Media Sanitization** technical capabilities Potential solutions for meeting these subcategory requirements include: Open-AudIT, LANSweeper, Spiceworks, OCSinventory-ng, AlienVault OSSIM, MS Excel (Manual), media sanitization tools. Solutions that were implemented in use cases: Open-AudIT DBAN
		PR.IP-7	**Low** Incorporate improvements derived from the monitoring, measurements, assessments, and lessons learned into protection process revisions. Ensure that the security plan for the manufacturing system facilitates the review, testing, and continual improvement of the security protection processes.	These subcategory requirements can be met by developing policies and procedures in the **Periodic Reevaluation of the Program** section of the **Security Program** document.
		PR.IP-8	**Low** Collaborate and share information about manufacturing system related security incidents and mitigation measures with designated sharing partners. Employ automated mechanisms where feasible to assist in information collaboration.	These subcategory requirements can be met by developing policies and procedures in the **Incident Response Policy** section of the **Incident Response** document.

Function	Category	Subcategory	Manufacturing Profile	Implementation Overview
			Low	
		PR.IP-9	Develop and maintain response and recovery plans that identify essential functions and associated contingency requirements, as well as providing a roadmap for implementing incident response. Plans should incorporate recovery objectives, restoration priorities, metrics, contingency roles, personnel assignments and contact information. Address maintaining essential functions despite system disruption, and the eventual restoration of the manufacturing system. Define incident types, resources and management support needed to effectively maintain and mature the incident response and contingency capabilities.	These subcategory requirements can be met by developing policies and procedures in the **Incident Response Plan and Incident Recovery Plan documents.**
			Low	
		PR.IP-10	Review response and recovery plans to determine the effectiveness of the plans, and the readiness to execute the plans.	These subcategory requirements can be met by developing policies and procedures in the **Incident Management** section of the **Security Program** document.
			Low	
	Information Protection Processes and Procedures (PR.IP)	PR.IP-11	Develop and maintain a personnel security program for the manufacturing system. Personnel security program should include policy, position risk designations, personnel screening, terminations and transfers, access agreements, third-party roles and responsibilities, and personnel sanctions.	These subcategory requirements can be met by developing policies and procedures in the **Security Program** document.
			Low	
PROTECT		PR.IP-12	Establish and maintain a process that allows continuous review of vulnerabilities, and defines strategies to mitigate them. Identify where manufacturing system vulnerabilities may be exposed to adversaries.	These subcategory requirements can be met by developing policies and procedures in the **Vulnerability Management** section of the **Procedures** document.

Function	Category	Subcategory	Manufacturing Profile	Implementation Overview
			Low	
			Schedule, perform, document and review records of maintenance and repairs on manufacturing system components.	Some of these subcategory requirements can be met by implementing solutions that provide the **Configuration Management, Change Control, Credential Management, Authentication and Authorization, Maintenance Tracking, and Physical Access Control** technical capabilities.
			Establish a process for maintenance personnel authorization, and escort non-authorized maintenance personnel.	
			Verify impacted security controls following maintenance or repairs.	Potential solutions for meeting these subcategory requirements include: Open-AudIT, I-doit, Salt, Puppet, Ansible, GRASSMARLIN, Wireshark, Microsoft Active Directory, FreeIPA, OCSinventory-ng, Fiix, Freshservice, and Microsoft Excel.
				Solutions that were implemented in use cases: Open-AudIT Microsoft Excel GRASSMARLIN Wireshark Microsoft Active Directory
PROTECT	**Maintenance (PR.MA)**	PR.MA-1		Some of these subcategory requirements can be met by developing policies and procedures in the **Physical Security** and **System Maintenance** section of the **Security Policy** document.

Function	Category	Subcategory	Manufacturing Profile	Implementation Overview
PROTECT	Maintenance (PR.MA)	PR.MA-2	**Low** Enforce approval requirements, control, and monitoring, of remote maintenance activities. Employ strong authenticators, record keeping, and session termination for remote maintenance.	Some of these subcategory requirements can be met by implementing solutions that provide the **Secure Remote Access, Credential Management, Authentication and Authorization, Network Monitoring, System Use Monitoring, and Maintenance Tracking** capabilities. Potential solutions for meeting these subcategory requirements include: VPN, Remote desktop, Microsoft Active Directory, FreeIPA, OCSinventory-ng, Fiix, Freshservice, Microsoft Excel, and Native operating system/device capabilities. Solutions that were implemented in use cases: Cisco AnyConnect VPN TeamViewer Microsoft Active Directory Microsoft Excel Native operating system/device capabilities.
	Protective Technology (PR.PT)	PR.PT-1	**Low** Generate audit records containing information that establishes what type of event occurred, when the event occurred, where the event occurred, the source of the event, the outcome of the event, and the identity of any individuals or manufacturing components associated with the event. Generate time stamps from an internal system clock that is mapped to Coordinated Universal Time (UTC) or Greenwich Mean Time (GMT). Enable authorized individuals to extend audit capabilities when required by events.	Some of these subcategory requirements can be met by developing policies and procedures in the **Remote Maintenance and System Maintenance** section of the **Security Policy** document These subcategory requirements can be met by implementing solutions that provide the **Time Synchronization, Physical Access Monitoring and Event Logging** technical capabilities. Potential solutions for meeting these subcategory requirements include: Native operating system/device capabilities, Electronic Access Control System, Sign in/out sheets, cameras, Graylog, Alienvault – OSSIM, SIEMonster Solutions that were implemented in use cases: Native operating system/device capabilities Electronic Access Control System Sign in/out sheets Graylog

Function	Category	Subcategory	Manufacturing Profile	Implementation Overview
		PR.PT-2	**Low** Employ safeguards to restrict the use of portable storage devices.	These subcategory requirements can be met by implementing solutions that provide the **Media Protection** technical capability. Potential solutions for meeting these subcategory requirements include: USB Port Locks, Native operating system/device capabilities. Solutions that were implemented in use cases: USB Port Locks
		PR.PT-3	**Low** Configure the manufacturing system to provide only essential capabilities	These subcategory requirements can be met by implementing solutions that provide the **Authentication and Authorization, and Ports and Services Lockdown** technical capabilities. Potential solutions for meeting these subcategory requirements include: Microsoft Active Directory, FreeIPA, Nmap, Native operating system/device capabilities Solutions that were implemented in use cases: Microsoft Active Directory Native operating system/device capabilities
PROTECT	Protective Technology (PR.PT)	PR.PT-4	**Low** Monitor and control communications at the external boundary and at key internal boundaries within the manufacturing system.	These subcategory requirements can be met by implementing solutions that provide the **Network Boundary Protection, Authentication and Authorization, and Network Monitoring** technical capabilities. Potential solutions for meeting these subcategory requirements include: firewalls, Security Onion, SNORT, Suricata, Zeek Network Security Monitor, Microsoft Active Directory, FreeIPA Solutions that were implemented in use cases: Microsoft Active Directory Security Onion Firewalls

CSF MFG PROFILE LOW SEC LVL EXAMPLE IG GENERAL IMPLEMENTATION GUIDANCE

Function	Category	Subcategory	Manufacturing Profile	Implementation Overview
			Low	
		DE.AE-1	Ensure that a baseline of network operations and expected data flows for the manufacturing system is developed, documented, and maintained to detect events.	These subcategory requirements can be met by implementing solutions that provide the **Baseline Establishment and Map Data Flows** technical capabilities.

Potential solutions for meeting these subcategory requirements include: Open-AudIT, GRASSMARLIN, Wireshark, I-doit, Salt, Puppet, Ansible, Microsoft Visio, and Ntopng

Solutions that were implemented in use cases:
Open-AudIT
GRASSMARLIN
Wireshark
Microsoft Visio |
| **DETECT** | **Anomalies and Events (DE.AE)** | | **Low** | |
| | | DE.AE-2 | Review and analyze detected events within the manufacturing system to understand attack targets and methods. | These subcategory requirements can be met by implementing solutions that provide the **Forensics** technical capability

Potential solutions for meeting these subcategory requirements include: Graylog, Wireshark, Security Onion, Zeek Network Security Monitor, CAINE (Computer Aided Investigative Environment)

Solutions that were implemented in use cases:
Graylog
Wireshark
Security Onion |
| | | | **Low** | |
| | | DE.AE-3 | Ensure that event data is compiled across the manufacturing system using various sources such as event reports, audit monitoring, network monitoring, physical access monitoring, and user/administrator reports. | These subcategory requirements can be met by implementing solutions that provide the **Event Logging** technical capability

Potential solutions for meeting these subcategory requirements include: Graylog, Alienvault – OSSIM, SIEMonster

Solutions that were implemented in use cases:
Graylog |

CSF Mfg Profile Low Sec Lvl Example IG General Implementation Guidance

Function	Category	Subcategory	Manufacturing Profile	Implementation Overview
DETECT	**Anomalies and Events (DE.AE)**	**DE.AE-4**	**Low** Determine negative impacts to manufacturing operations, assets, and individuals resulting from detected events, and correlate with risk assessment outcomes.	These subcategory requirements can be met by developing policies and procedures in the **Event Impacts** section of the **Procedures** document
		DE.AE-5	**Low** Define incident alert thresholds for the manufacturing system.	Some of these subcategory requirements can be met by developing policies and procedures in the **Incident Alert Thresholds** section of the **Incident Response** document
	Security Continuous Monitoring (DE.CM)	**DE.CM-1**	**Low** Conduct ongoing security status monitoring of the manufacturing system network to detect defined cybersecurity events and indicators of potential cybersecurity events. Detect unauthorized local, network, and remote connections, and identify unauthorized use of the manufacturing system. Generate audit records for defined cybersecurity events. Monitor network communications at the external boundary of the system and at key internal boundaries within the system. Heighten system monitoring activity whenever there is an indication of increased risk.	Some of these subcategory requirements can be met by implementing solutions that provide the **Network Boundary Protection, Network Monitoring, and Event Logging** technical capabilities. Potential solutions for meeting these subcategory requirements include: firewalls, Security Onion, SNORT, Suricata, Zeek Network Security Monitor Graylog, Alienvault – OSSIM, SIEMonster Solutions that were implemented in use cases: Firewalls Security Onion Graylog
		DE.CM-2	**Low** Conduct ongoing security status monitoring of the manufacturing system facility to detect physical security incidents.	Some of these subcategory requirements can be met by developing policies and procedures in the **Continuous Monitoring** section of the **Security Policy** document These subcategory requirements can be met by implementing solutions that provide the **Physical Access Monitoring** technical capability Potential solutions for meeting these subcategory requirements include: electronic access control systems, cameras, Sign in/out sheets Solutions that were implemented in use cases: Electronic access control system Sign in/out sheet

Function	Category	Subcategory	Manufacturing Profile	Implementation Overview
		DE.CM-3	**Low** Conduct security status monitoring of personnel activity associated with the manufacturing system. Enforce software usage and installation restrictions.	These subcategory requirements can be met by implementing solutions that provide the **Authentication and Authorization, System Use Monitoring, and Physical Access Monitoring** technical capabilities. Potential solutions for meeting these subcategory requirements include: Microsoft Active Directory, FreeIPA, Symantec Endpoint Protection, Native operating system/device capabilities, electronic access control systems, cameras, Sign in/out sheets Solutions that were implemented in use cases: Active Directory Symantec Endpoint Protection Native operating system/device capabilities Electronic access control system Sign in/out sheet
DETECT	Security Continuous Monitoring (DE.CM)	DE.CM-4	**Low** Deploy malicious code protection mechanisms throughout the manufacturing system where safe and feasible to detect and eradicate malicious code. Update malicious code protection mechanisms whenever new releases are available in accordance with the configuration management policy and procedures for the manufacturing system.	These subcategory requirements can be met by implementing solutions that provide the **Anti-virus/malware and Vulnerability Management** technical capabilities. Potential solutions for meeting these subcategory requirements include: Symantec Endpoint Protection, ClamAV, NamicSoft, OpenVAS, Tenable Nessus Solutions that were implemented in use cases: Symantec Endpoint Protection NamicSoft
		DE.CM-5	**Low** None	N/A

CSF MFG PROFILE LOW SEC LVL EXAMPLE IG GENERAL IMPLEMENTATION GUIDANCE

Function	Category	Subcategory	Manufacturing Profile	Implementation Overview
			Low	These subcategory requirements can be met by implementing solutions that provide the **Network Monitoring and Event Logging** technical capabilities.
		DE.CM-6	Conduct ongoing security status monitoring of external service provider activity on the manufacturing system.	
			Detect defined cybersecurity events and indicators of potential cybersecurity events from external service providers.	Potential solutions for meeting these subcategory requirements include: Security Onion, SNORT, Suricata, Zeek Network Security Monitor, Graylog, Alienvault – OSSIM, SIEMonster
			Monitor compliance of external providers with personnel security policies and procedures, and contract security requirements.	Solutions that were implemented in use cases: Security Onion Graylog
DETECT	**Security Continuous Monitoring (DE.CM)**		**Low**	These subcategory requirements can be met by implementing solutions that provide the **Hardware Inventory, Software Inventory, Systems Development Lifecycle Management, Baseline Establishment, Change Control, and Network Monitoring** technical capabilities.
		DE.CM-7	Conduct ongoing security status monitoring on the manufacturing system for unauthorized personnel, connections, devices, access points, and software.	
			Monitor for system inventory discrepancies.	Potential solutions for meeting these subcategory requirements include: Open-AudIT, LANSweeper, Spiceworks, OCSinventory-ng, AlienVault OSSIM, Microsoft Excel (Manual), I-doit, Salt, Puppet, Ansible, GRASSMARLIN, Wireshark, Security Onion, SNORT, Suricata, Zeek Network Security Monitor
			Deploy monitoring devices strategically within the manufacturing system to collect essential information to detect specific events of interest.	Solutions that were implemented in use cases: Open-AudIT GRASSMARLIN Wireshark Microsoft Excel Security Onion

Function	Category	Subcategory	Manufacturing Profile	Implementation Overview
DETECT	Security Continuous Monitoring (DE.CM)	DE.CM-8	**Low** Conduct vulnerability scans on the manufacturing system where safe and feasible. Include analysis, remediation, and information sharing in the vulnerability scanning process. Employ control system-specific vulnerability scanning tools and techniques where safe and feasible. Active vulnerability scanning, which introduces network traffic, is used with care on manufacturing systems to ensure that system functions are not adversely impacted by the scanning process.	Some of these subcategory requirements can be met by implementing solutions that provide the **Vulnerability Scanning** capability. Potential solutions for meeting these subcategory requirements include: Tenable Nessus, OpenVAS, AlienVault OSSIM Solutions that were implemented in use cases: Tenable Nessus Some subcategory requirements can be met by developing policies and procedures in the **Vulnerability Management Process** section of the **Security Procedures** document
		DE.DP-1	**Low** Define roles and responsibilities for detection activities on the manufacturing system and ensure accountability.	These subcategory requirements can be met by developing policies and procedures in the **Role-based Security Responsibilities** section of the **Security Policy** document.
		DE.DP-2	**Low** Conduct detection activities in accordance with applicable federal and state laws, industry regulations and standards, policies, and other applicable requirements.	These subcategory requirements can be met by developing policies and procedures in the **Continuous Monitoring** section of the **Security Policy** document.
	Detection Processes (DE.DP)	DE.DP-3	**Low, Moderate and High** Validate that event detection processes are operating as intended.	These subcategory requirements can be met by implementing solutions that provide the **Event Logging** technical capability Potential solutions for meeting these subcategory requirements include: Graylog, Alienvault – OSSIM, SIEMonster Solutions that were implemented in use cases: Graylog

CSF Mfg Profile Low Sec Lvl Example IG General Implementation Guidance

Function	Category	Subcategory	Manufacturing Profile	Implementation Overview
DETECT		DE.DP-4	**Low** Communicate event detection information to defined personnel. Event detection information includes for example, alerts on atypical account usage, unauthorized remote access, wireless connectivity, mobile device connection, altered configuration settings, contrasting system component inventory, use of maintenance tools and nonlocal maintenance, physical access, temperature and humidity, equipment delivery and removal, communications at the information system boundaries, use of mobile code, use of VoIP, and malware disclosure.	These subcategory requirements can be met by developing policies and procedures in the **Continuous Monitoring** section of the **Security Policy** document.
	Detection Processes (DE.DP)	DE.DP-5	**Low** Incorporate improvements derived from the monitoring, measurements, assessments, and lessons learned into detection process revisions. Ensure the security plan for the manufacturing system provides for the review, testing, and continual improvement of the security detection processes.	These subcategory requirements can be met by developing policies and procedures in the **Incident Management and Periodic Reevaluation of the Program** section of the **Security Program** document.
RESPOND	**Response Planning (RS.RP)**	RS.RP-1	**Low** Execute the response plan during or after a cybersecurity event on the manufacturing system.	These subcategory requirements can be met by developing policies and procedures in the **Purpose** section of the **Incident Response** document.
	Communications (RS.CO)	RS.CO-1	**Low** Ensure personnel understand objectives, restoration priorities, task sequences and assignment responsibilities for event response.	These subcategory requirements can be met by developing policies and procedures in the **Incident Response Policy** section of the **Incident Response** document.

Function	Category	Subcategory	Manufacturing Profile	Implementation Overview
RESPOND	Communications (RS.CO)	RS.CO-2	**Low** Employ prompt reporting to appropriate stakeholders for cybersecurity events on the manufacturing system. Ensure that cybersecurity events on the manufacturing system are reported consistent with the response plan.	These subcategory requirements can be met by developing policies and procedures in the **Guidelines for Reporting to Stake Holders** section of the **Incident Response** document.
		RS.CO-3	**Low** Share cybersecurity incident information with relevant stakeholders per the response plan.	These subcategory requirements can be met by developing policies and procedures in the **Incident Response Policy** section of the **Incident Response** document.
		RS.CO-4	**Low** Coordinate cybersecurity incident response actions with all relevant stakeholders. Stakeholders for incident response include for example, mission/business owners, manufacturing system owners, integrators, vendors, human resources offices, physical and personnel security offices, legal departments, operations personnel, and procurement offices.	These subcategory requirements can be met by developing policies and procedures in the **Incident Response Policy** section of the **Incident Response** document.
		RS.CO-5	**Low** Share cybersecurity event information voluntarily, as appropriate, with industry security groups to achieve broader cybersecurity situational awareness. For example, the DHS National Cybersecurity & Communications Integration Center (NCCIC) [6] serves as a centralized location where operational elements involved in cybersecurity and communications reliance are coordinated and integrated. The Industrial Control Systems Cyber Emergency Response Team (ICS-CERT) [7] collaborates with international and private sector Computer Emergency Response Teams (CERTs) to share control systems-related cybersecurity incidents and mitigation measures.	These subcategory requirements can be met by developing policies and procedures in the **Continuous Monitoring** section of the **Security Policy** document.

Function	Category	Subcategory	Manufacturing Profile	Implementation Overview
RESPOND	**Analysis (RS.AN)**	**RS.AN-1**	**Low** Investigate cybersecurity-related notifications generated from detection systems.	These subcategory requirements can be met by developing policies and procedures in the **Response** section of the **Security Procedures** document and **Incident Response Policy** section of the **Incident Response Plan** document.
		RS.AN-2	**Low** Understand the full implication of the cybersecurity incident based on thorough investigation and analysis results. Correlate detected event information and incident responses with risk assessment outcomes to achieve perspective on incident impact across the organization.	These subcategory requirements can be met by developing policies and procedures in the **Incident Response Policy** section of the **Incident Response Plan** document.
		RS.AN-3	**Low** Conduct forensic analysis on collected cybersecurity event information to determine root cause.	These subcategory requirements can be met by implementing solutions that provide the **Event Logging and Forensics** technical capabilities. Potential solutions for meeting these subcategory requirements include: Graylog, Wireshark, Zeek Network Security Monitor, CAINE (Computer Aided Investigative Environment), Alienvault – OSSIM, SIEMonster, Security Onion Solutions that were implemented in use cases: Graylog Wireshark Security Onion
		RS.AN-4	**Low** Categorize cybersecurity incidents according to level of severity and impact consistent with the response plan.	These subcategory requirements can be met by developing policies and procedures in the **Categories of Incidents** section of the **Incident Response Plan** document.

Function	Category	Subcategory	Manufacturing Profile	Implementation Overview
RESPOND	Mitigation (RS.MI)	RS.MI-1	**Low** Contain cybersecurity incidents to minimize impact on the manufacturing system.	These subcategory requirements can be met by developing policies and procedures in the **Incident Response Workflow** section of the **Incident Response Plan** document.
		RS.MI-2	**Low** Mitigate cybersecurity incidents occurring on the manufacturing system.	These subcategory requirements can be met by implementing solutions that provide the **Incident Management** technical capability Potential solutions for meeting these subcategory requirements include: Sandia Cyber Omni Tracker (SCOT), The Hive Project, Request Tracker Incident Response (RTIR) Solutions that were implemented in use cases: The Hive Project
		RS.MI-3	**Low** Ensure that vulnerabilities identified while responding to a cybersecurity incident are mitigated or documented as accepted risks.	These subcategory requirements can be met by implementing solutions that provide the **Vulnerability Management and Incident Management** technical capabilities. Potential solutions for meeting these subcategory requirements include: NamicSoft, OpenVAS, Tenable Nessus, AlienVault OSSIM, Sandia Cyber Omni Tracker (SCOT), The Hive Project, Request Tracker Incident Response (RTIR) Solutions that were implemented in use cases: NamicSoft The Hive Project

Function	Category	Subcategory	Manufacturing Profile	Implementation Overview
RESPOND		RS.IM-1	**Low** Incorporate lessons learned from ongoing incident handling activities into incident response procedures, training, and testing, and implement the resulting changes accordingly.	These subcategory requirements can be met by developing policies and procedures in the **Incident Response Policy** section of the **Incident Response** document.
	Improvements (RS.IM)	RS.IM-2	**Low** Update the response plans to address changes to the organization, manufacturing system, attack vectors, or environment of operation and problems encountered during plan implementation, execution, or testing. Updates may include, for example, responses to disruptions or failures, and predetermined procedures. Enable a process for the response plan to evolve to reflect new threats, improved technology, and lessons learned.	These subcategory requirements can be met by developing policies and procedures in the **Incident Response Policy** section of the **Incident Response** document.
RECOVER	Recovery Planning (RC.RP)	RC.RP-1	**Low** Execute the recovery plan during or after a cybersecurity incident on the manufacturing system. Restore the manufacturing system within a predefined time-period from configuration-controlled and integrity-protected information representing a known, operational state for the components.	These subcategory requirements can be met by developing policies and procedures in the **Objectives, and RPO and RTO Targets** section of the **Recovery Plan** document.
	Improvements (RC.IM)	RC.IM-1	**Low** Incorporate lessons learned from ongoing recovery activities into system recovery procedures, training, and testing, and implement the resulting changes accordingly.	These subcategory requirements can be met by developing policies and procedures in the **Plan Testing and Maintenance** section of the **Recovery Plan** document.

Function	Category	Subcategory	Manufacturing Profile	Implementation Overview
RECOVER	Improvements (RC.IM)	RC.IM-2	**Low** Update the recovery plan to address changes to the organization, manufacturing system, or environment of operation and problems encountered during plan implementation, execution, or testing. Ensure that updates are integrated into the recovery plans.	These subcategory requirements can be met by developing policies and procedures in the **Plan Testing and Maintenance** section of the **Recovery Plan** document.
	Communications (RC.CO)	RC.CO-1	**Low** Centralize and coordinate information distribution, and manage the public facing representation of the organization. Public relations management may include, for example, managing media interactions, coordinating and logging all requests for interviews, handling and 'triaging' phone calls and e-mail requests, matching media requests with appropriate and available internal experts who are ready to be interviewed, screening all of information provided to the media, ensuring personnel are familiar with public relations and privacy policies.	These subcategory requirements can be met by developing policies and procedures in the **Communications** section of the **Recovery Plan** document.
		RC.CO-2	**Low** Employ a crisis response strategy to protect against negative impact and repair organizational reputation. Crisis response strategies include, for example, actions to shape attributions of the crisis, change perceptions of the organization in crisis, and reduce the negative effect generated by the crisis.	These subcategory requirements can be met by developing policies and procedures in the **Communications** section of the **Recovery Plan** document.
		RC.CO-3	**Low** Communicate recovery activities to all relevant stakeholders, and executive and management teams.	These subcategory requirements can be met by developing policies and procedures in the **Communication** section of the **Recovery Plan** document.

1167   **8.   Laboratory Environment Overview**

1168   This section provides details on the laboratory environment (i.e., lab), located on the NIST main
1169   campus in Gaithersburg, Maryland. The lab contains a shared infrastructure of networked
1170   servers, measurement tools, industrial robots, hardware-in-the-loop simulators, and other
1171   technologies to support the Manufacturing Profile implementation on the two manufacturing
1172   systems: a Process Control System (PCS) [12] and a Collaborative Robotics System (CRS) [11].
1173   The PCS and CRS employ real-world industrial hardware (e.g., programmable logic controllers),
1174   networking devices, and protocols to emulate a process and discrete manufacturing system,
1175   respectively. Further details on two systems are described in Section 8.1 and Section 8.2.

1176   The network infrastructure, shown in Figure 8-1, is used for many research functions including:
1177   testing, deployment, and hosting of cybersecurity tools, measurement systems for network
1178   traffic, creation and manipulation of network traffic for inducing anomalous network activity,
1179   and archival storage of experiment data. A virtualization environment was implemented to
1180   support the numerous cybersecurity technologies and tools required for the implementation.

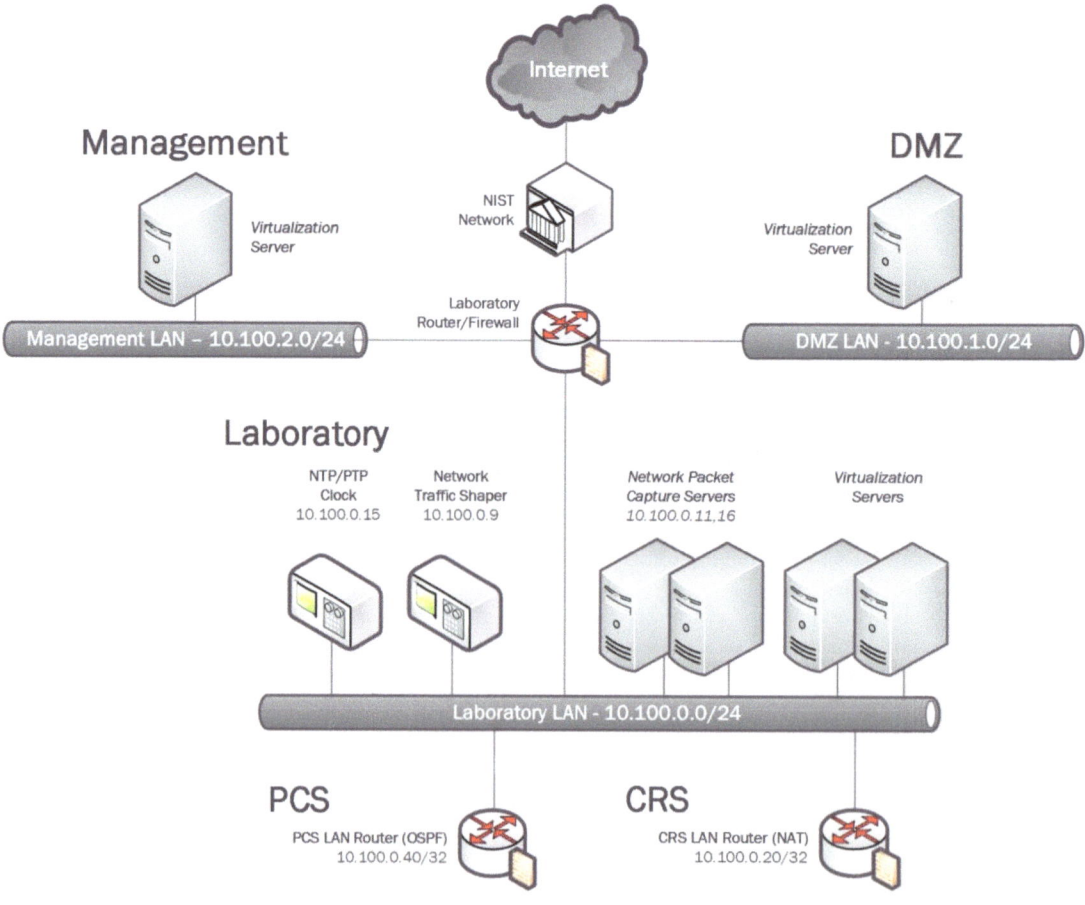

1181

1182   **Figure 8-1 Lab Network Infrastructure**

1183   The lab network infrastructure is separated into three independent network zones: Management
1184   zone, DMZ (Demilitarized Zone), and Laboratory zone. The Management zone contains hosts

1185   that are used to manage the numerous laboratory devices (e.g., network hardware, virtualization
1186   servers). The DMZ zone contains hosts that perform data-sharing functions between the lab
1187   network and the top-level network (in this case, the NIST Network). And the Laboratory zone
1188   contains the shared measurement servers and tools, and a virtualization infrastructure for hosting
1189   cybersecurity tools.

1190   Attached to the Laboratory zone are the local PCS and CRS networks, which operate
1191   independently of each other. The PCS network accesses the Laboratory LAN using the Open
1192   Shortest Path First (OSPF) routing protocol, and the CRS access the Laboratory LAN using
1193   Dynamic Network Address Translation (Dynamic NAT).

1194   A dedicated network packet capture server is provided for both the PCS and CRS. Packets are
1195   captured using two methods: packet mirroring, and bump-in-the-wire network probes. Packet
1196   mirroring involves configuring network devices (e.g., routers, switches) to duplicate and forward
1197   the packet to another port. Network probes perform a similar function, but they must be
1198   physically connected to the network cable. In the lab, mirrored packets are aggregated into two
1199   streams (one containing PCS traffic, and the other containing CRS traffic) using a packet broker.
1200   Network traffic from the aggregator and network probes terminate at the network packet capture
1201   servers, where they are buffered, stored, and later processed to calculate the metrics and KPI
1202   required for experimental analysis.

1203   **8.1 Process-based Manufacturing System**

1204   The Process Control System emulates an industrial continuous manufacturing system, a
1205   manufacturing process to produce or process materials continuously, where the materials are
1206   moving, going through chemical reactions, or undergoing mechanical or thermal treatment
1207   continuously. Continuous manufacturing usually implies a 24x7 operation with infrequent
1208   maintenance shutdowns and is contrasted with batch manufacturing. Examples of continuous
1209   manufacturing systems include chemical production, oil refining, natural gas processing, and
1210   waste water treatment.

1211   The system uses the Tennessee Eastman challenge problem [9] a real-world industrial chemical
1212   manufacturing process, as the simulation model for the chemical reaction. The system integrates
1213   the control algorithm developed by Ricker [10] to control the simulated chemical reaction. With
1214   the use of widely deployed industrial hardware like programmable logic controllers (PLCs) and
1215   industrial network switches as part of the control loop, this system emulates a complete setup of
1216   a continuous chemical manufacturing system. This hardware-in-the-loop setup allows the testbed
1217   to measure the performance of the manufacturing system using real-world industrial hardware
1218   devices, while the chemical manufacturing process is simulated in software.

1219
1220
1221   **Figure 8-2 PCS System**

1222
1223   ### 8.1.1 Control System Operation

1224   The Process Control System includes a software simulator to emulate the Tennessee Eastman
1225   chemical reaction process. The simulator is written in C code and is executed on a Windows 7
1226   based computer. In addition, the system includes a Programmable Logic Controller (PLC), a
1227   software controller implemented in MATLAB, a human-machine interface (HMI), an Object
1228   Linking and Embedding for Process Control (OPC) Data Access (DA) server, a Data Historian,
1229   an engineering workstation, and several virtual Local Area Network (LAN) switches and
1230   network routers. The Process Control System is housed in a 19-inch rack system, shown in
1231   Figure 8-2.

1232   The Tennessee Eastman Plant Simulator requires a controller to provide a control loop in order
1233   to operate continuously. A decentralized controller implemented in Simulink, developed by
1234   Ricker [10] is used as the process controller. The Ricker implementation matches the Plant
1235   Simulator accurately, and the controller is a separate software process that runs on a separate
1236   computer from the Plant Simulator.

1237   To provide communication between the Plant Simulator and the Controller, a hardware
1238   Programmable Logic Controller (PLC) with industrial network protocol capability is used. The
1239   industrial protocol is used to communicate between the Plant Simulator and the PLC. The Plant
1240   Simulator sends its sensor information to the Controller, and the Controller algorithm uses the
1241   sensor inputs to compute the desired values of the actuators and sends them back to the Plant
1242   Simulator.

1243

1244 In the Plant Simulator computer, a multi-node DeviceNet card was installed. DeviceNet is a
1245 common industrial protocol used in the automation industry to exchange data between control
1246 devices. The multi-node card allows a single hardware device to emulate multiple virtual
1247 DeviceNet nodes. In our case, each sensor and actuator point is a dedicated node. Therefore, 53
1248 virtual nodes (41 for sensors and 12 for actuators) were configured in the system. A software
1249 interface was developed to send and receive sensor and actuator values between the Plant
1250 Simulator and the PLC through DeviceNet.

1251 An OPC DA Server is running in a Windows 7 computer, acting as the main data gateway for the
1252 PLC. The PLC communicates to the OPC DA server to update and retrieve all the sensor and
1253 actuator information, respectively. This sensor and actuator information is also known as a "tag"
1254 in PLC terminology. The Controller has a MATLAB Simulink interface that communicates with
1255 the OPC DA server directly.

1256 A Human-Machine Interface (HMI) and a Data Historian are implemented in the system. The
1257 HMI provides a graphical user interface to present information to an operator or user about the
1258 state of the process. The Data Historian serves as the main database to record all the process
1259 sensor and actuator information. Both HMI and Data Historian have built-in interfaces to
1260 establish connections to the OPC DA to access all the process information.

1261 An engineering workstation is used in the system for engineering support, such as PLC
1262 development and control, HMI development and deployment, and Data Historian data retrieval.

1263 **8.1.2 Network Architecture**

1264 The Process Control System network is segmented from the main Testbed network by a
1265 boundary router. The router is using a dynamic routing protocol, Open Shortest Path First
1266 (OSPF), to communicate with the main tested router. The network architecture is shown in
1267 Figure 8-3.

1268 All network traffic needs to go through the boundary router to access the main testbed network.

1269 There are two virtual network segments in the system. Each network is managed by an Ethernet
1270 switch. The HMI and the Controller are in virtual network VLAN-1, while the Plant Simulator,
1271 Data Historian, OPC DA Server, and PLC are in virtual network VLAN-2.

1272 VLAN-1 simulates a central control room environment that the HMI and the controllers are
1273 virtually located in the same network segment. VLAN-2 simulates the process operation
1274 environment which typically consists of the operating plant, PLCs, OPC server, and the Data
1275 Historian.

1276

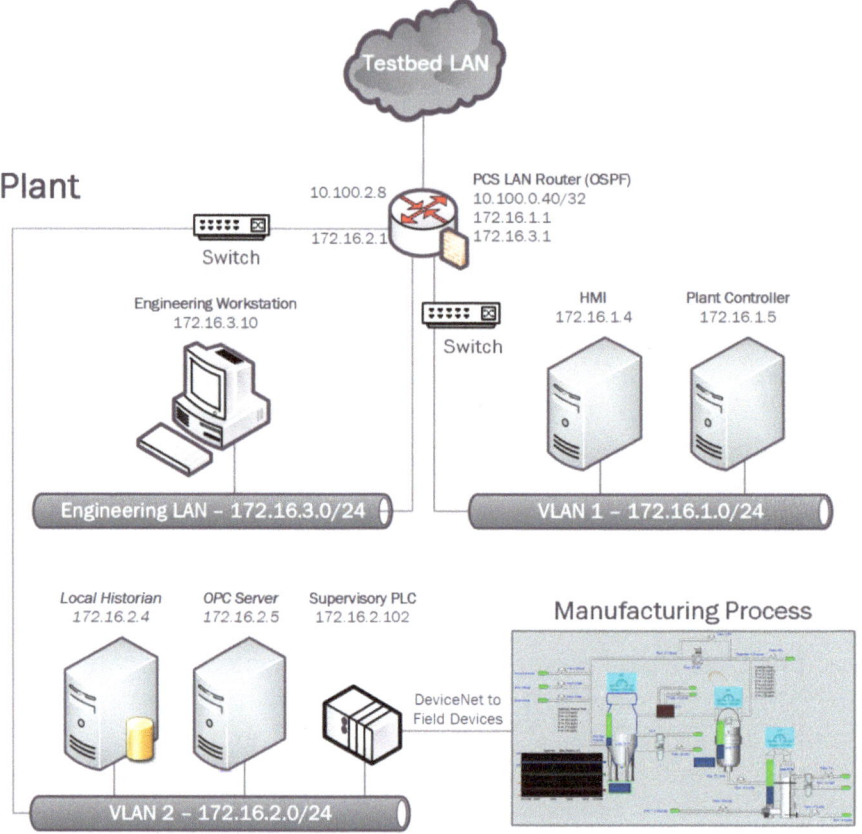

1277

1278   **Figure 8-3 PCS Network Architecture**

1279

1280   8.2   Discrete-based Manufacturing System

1281   The CRS workcell, shown in Figure 8-4 contains two robotic arms that perform a material
1282   handling process called machine tending [11]. Robotic machine tending utilizes robots to interact
1283   with machinery, performing physical operations a human operator would normally perform (e.g.,
1284   loading and unloading of parts in a machine, opening and closing of machine doors, activating
1285   operator control panel buttons, etc.).

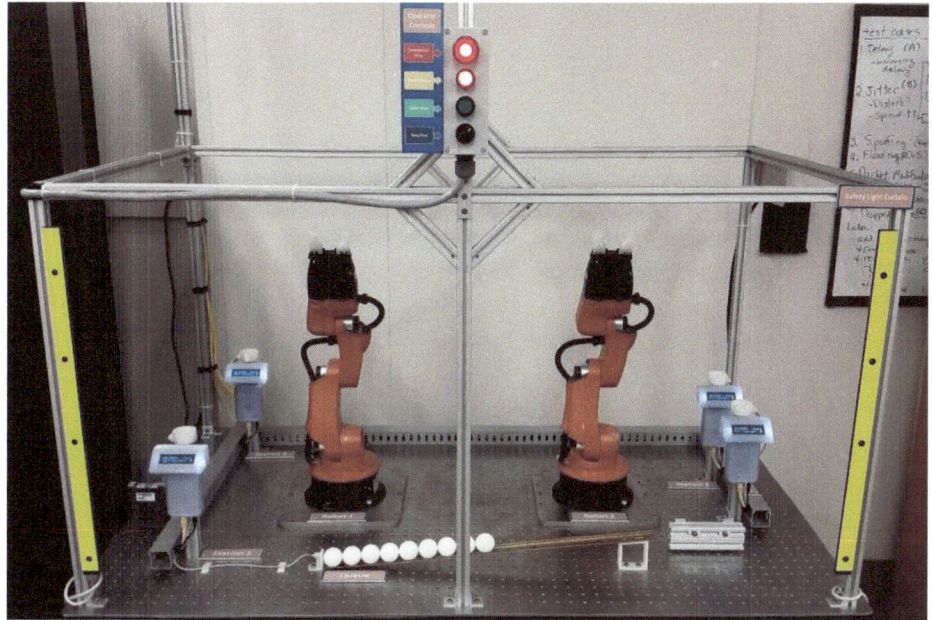

1286

1287　**Figure 8-4 The CRS workcell in standby, waiting for the operator to initiate the manufacturing process. The**
1288　**operator control panel is visible at the top of the figure.**

1289　A human operator interfaces with the workcell through a human-machine interface (HMI) and a
1290　control panel external to the work area.

1291　The workcell was designed and constructed to be reconfigurable, allowing numerous types of
1292　operational methodologies, network topologies, and industrial networking protocols to be
1293　investigated. The two robots collaborate to transport parts through the manufacturing process, as
1294　a single robot cannot physically reach all four stations. Having two robots also increases
1295　workcell efficiency.

1296　### 8.2.1　Control System Operation

1297　Parts are moved by the robot arms through four simulated machining operations, known as
1298　*stations*. Each station is comprised of: a fixture for holding the part, an infrared proximity sensor
1299　for detecting the part, a single board computer simulating the actions and communications of a
1300　typical machining center, and a liquid crystal display (LCD) for displaying the operational status
1301　of the station. The stations communicate with the supervisory programmable logic controller
1302　(PLC) over the workcell local area network (LAN). The supervisory PLC monitors and controls
1303　all aspects of the manufacturing process.

1304　Manufacturing data from the four machining stations are used by the PLC to determine which
1305　operations (known as *jobs*) the robots must perform to keep the parts moving through the
1306　sequential manufacturing process. The PLC also communicates with the HMI for operator
1307　visibility and control.

1308　The workcell is supported by a shared infrastructure of networked servers, measurement tools,
1309　and other technologies. The infrastructure is used for many research functions including: testing,
1310　deployment, and hosting of cybersecurity tools; measurement and packet capture systems for

1311   network traffic; creation and manipulation of network traffic for inducing anomalous network
1312   activity; and archival storage of experiment data. A virtualized server infrastructure was installed
1313   to support the numerous cybersecurity technologies and tools required for the implementation.

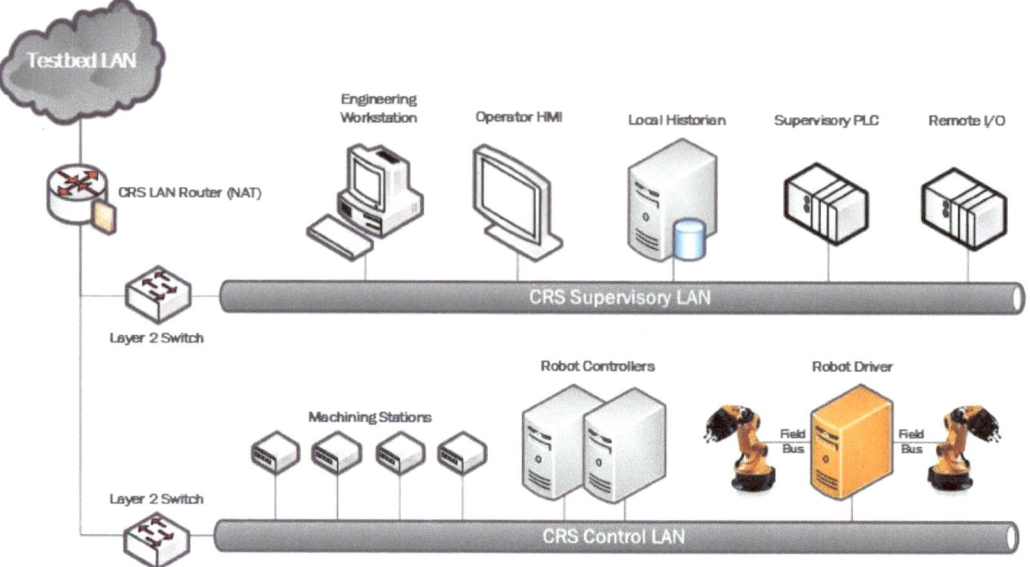

1314

1315   **Figure 8-5 Robotic Assembly CRS Network**

1316   ## 8.2.2   Network Architecture

1317   The CRS network, shown in Figure 8-5, is hierarchically architected, separating the devices
1318   performing supervisory functions from the devices controlling the manufacturing process. The
1319   workcell top-level router is a Siemens RUGGEDCOM RX1510, and provides firewall
1320   capabilities for rule-based allowance and restriction of network traffic. The router is connected to
1321   the Testbed LAN using network address translation (NAT). Layer 2 network traffic for the
1322   Supervisory LAN is handled by a Netgear GS724T managed Ethernet switch, and network traffic
1323   for the Control LAN is handled by a Siemens i800 managed Ethernet switch.

1324   The router and network switches are configured to mirror all incoming network traffic to a
1325   packet capture server located in the measurement rack. In-line (i.e., *bump-in-the-wire*) network
1326   taps are located at the PLC, HMI, and Station 1 to provide dedicated forwarding of all incoming
1327   and outgoing network traffic to the packet capture server.

1328   All manufacturing process-based network communications utilize the Modbus TCP industrial
1329   network protocol, and all network traffic between the robot controllers and robot drivers utilize
1330   the Robot Operating System's (ROS) native transport protocols TCPROS and UDPROS.

1331 ## Appendix A - Acronyms and Abbreviations

1332 Selected acronyms and abbreviations used in in this document are defined below.

1333 **CAN** Controller Area Network

1334 **CSF** Cybersecurity Framework

1335 **FIPS** Federal Information Processing Standards

1336 **HMI** Human Machine Interface

1337 **ICS** Industrial Control System

1338 **ICS-CERT** Industrial Control Systems Cyber Emergency Response Team

1339 **IEC** International Electrotechnical Commission

1340 **ISA** The International Society of Automation

1341 **IT** Information Technology

1342 **LAN** Local Area Network

1343 **NCCIC** National Cybersecurity & Communications Integration Center

1344 **NIST** National Institute of Standards and Technology

1345 **OT** Operational Technology

1346 **PLC** Programmable Logic Controller

1347 **TCPROS** TCP based Robot Operating System protocol

1348 **UDPROS** TCP based Robot Operating System protocol

1349 **US-CERT** United States Computer Emergency Readiness Team

1350 **VPN** Virtual Private Network

1351 **Appendix B - Glossary**

1352   Selected terms used in in this document are defined below.

1353   **Actuator** - A device for moving or controlling a mechanism or system. It is operated by a source
1354   of energy, typically electric current, hydraulic fluid pressure, or pneumatic pressure, and converts
1355   that energy into motion. An actuator is the mechanism by which a control system acts upon an
1356   environment. The control system can be simple (a fixed mechanical or electronic system),
1357   software-based (e.g. a printer driver, robot control system), or a human or other agent.   [800-82]
1358
1359   **Business/Mission Objectives** - Broad expression of business goals. Specified target outcome
1360   for business operations.
1361
1362   **Category** - The subdivision of a Function into groups of cybersecurity outcomes closely tied to
1363   programmatic needs and particular activities.
1364
1365   **Critical Infrastructure** - Essential services and related assets that underpin American society
1366   and serve as the backbone of the nation's economy, security, and health. [DHS]
1367
1368   **Criticality Reviews** - A determination of the ranking and priority of manufacturing system
1369   components, services, processes, and inputs in order to establish operational thresholds and
1370   recovery objectives.
1371
1372   **Critical Services** - The subset of mission essential services required to conduct manufacturing
1373   operations. Function or capability that is required to maintain health, safety, the environment and
1374   availability for the equipment under control. [62443]
1375
1376   **Cyber Risk** - Risk of financial loss, operational disruption, or damage, from the failure of the
1377   digital technologies employed for informational and/or operational functions introduced to a
1378   manufacturing system via electronic means from the unauthorized access, use, disclosure,
1379   disruption, modification, or destruction of the manufacturing system.
1380
1381   **Cybersecurity** - The process of protecting information by preventing, detecting, and responding
1382   to attacks.   [CSF]
1383
1384   **Event** - Any observable occurrence on a manufacturing system. Events can include
1385   cybersecurity changes that may have an impact on manufacturing operations (including mission,
1386   capabilities, or reputation). [CSF]
1387
1388   **Firmware** - Software program or set of instructions programmed on the flash ROM of a
1389   hardware device. It provides the necessary instructions for how the device communicates with
1390   the other computer hardware. [Techterms.com]
1391
1392   **Framework** - The Cybersecurity Framework developed for defining protection of critical
1393   infrastructure. It provides a common language for understanding, managing, and expressing

1394 cybersecurity risk both internally and externally. Includes activities to achieve specific
1395 cybersecurity outcomes, and references examples of guidance to achieve those outcomes.
1396
1397 **Function** - Primary unit within the Cybersecurity Framework. Exhibits basic cybersecurity
1398 activities at their highest level.
1399
1400 **Incident** - An occurrence that actually or potentially jeopardizes the confidentiality, integrity, or
1401 availability of an information system or the information the system processes, stores, or transmits
1402 or that constitutes a violation or imminent threat of violation of security policies, security
1403 procedures, or acceptable use policies. [CSF]
1404
1405 **Informative References** - Specific sections of standards, guidelines, and practices common
1406 among critical infrastructure sectors that illustrate a method to achieve the outcomes associated
1407 with each Subcategory in the Cybersecurity Framework.
1408
1409 **Manufacturing Operations** - Activities concerning the facility operation, system processes,
1410 materials input/output, maintenance, supply and distribution, health, and safety, emergency
1411 response, human resources, security, information technology and other contributing measures to
1412 the manufacturing enterprise.
1413
1414 **Network Access** - any access across a network connection in lieu of local access (i.e., user being
1415 physically present at the device).
1416
1417 **Operational technology** - Hardware and software that detects or causes a change through the
1418 direct monitoring and/or control of physical devices, processes and events in the enterprise.
1419 [Gartner.com]
1420
1421 **Programmable Logic Controller** - A solid-state control system that has a user-programmable
1422 memory for storing instructions for the purpose of implementing specific functions such as I/O
1423 control, logic, timing, counting, three mode (PID) control, communication, arithmetic, and data
1424 and file processing. [800-82]
1425
1426 **Profile** - A representation of the outcomes that a particular system or organization has selected
1427 from the Framework Categories and Subcategories. [CSF]
1428 - Target Profile - the desired outcome or 'to be' state of cybersecurity implementation
1429 - Current Profile – the 'as is' state of system cybersecurity
1430
1431 **Protocol** - A set of rules (i.e., formats and procedures) to implement and control some type of
1432 association (e.g., communication) between systems. [800-82]
1433
1434 **Remote Access** - Access by users (or information systems) communicating external to an
1435 information system security perimeter. Network access is any access across a network
1436 connection in lieu of local access (i.e., user being physically present at the device). [800-53]
1437
1438 **Resilience Requirements** - The business-driven availability and reliability characteristics for the
1439 manufacturing system that specify recovery tolerances from disruptions and major incidents.

1440 **Risk Assessment** - The process of identifying risks to agency operations (including mission,
1441 functions, image, or reputation), agency assets, or individuals by determining the probability of
1442 occurrence, the resulting impact, and additional security controls that would mitigate this impact.
1443 Part of risk management, synonymous with risk analysis. Incorporates threat and vulnerability
1444 analyses. [800-82]
1445

1446 **Risk Tolerance** - The level of risk that the Manufacturer is willing to accept in pursuit of
1447 strategic goals and objectives. [800-53]
1448

1449 **Router** - A computer that is a gateway between two networks at OSI layer 3 and that relays and
1450 directs data packets through that inter-network. The most common form of router operates on IP
1451 packets. [800-82]
1452

1453 **Security Control** - The management, operational, and technical controls (i.e., safeguards or
1454 countermeasures) prescribed for a system to protect the confidentiality, integrity, and availability
1455 of the system, its components, processes, and data. [800-82]
1456

1457 **Subcategory** - The subdivision of a Category into specific outcomes of technical and/or
1458 management activities. Examples of Subcategories include "External information systems are
1459 catalogued," "Data-at-rest is protected," and "Notifications from detection systems are
1460 investigated." [CSF]
1461

1462 **Supporting Services** - Providers of external system services to the manufacturer through a
1463 variety of consumer-producer relationships including but not limited to: joint ventures; business
1464 partnerships; outsourcing arrangements (i.e., through contracts, interagency agreements, lines of
1465 business arrangements); licensing agreements; and/or supply chain exchanges. Supporting
1466 services include, for example, Telecommunications, engineering services, power, water,
1467 software, tech support, and security. [800-53]
1468

1469 **Switch** - A device that channels incoming data from any of multiple input ports to the specific
1470 output port that will take the data toward its intended destination. [Whatis.com]
1471

1472 **System Categorization** - The characterization of a manufacturing system, its components, and
1473 operations, based on an assessment of the potential impact that a loss of availability, integrity, or
1474 confidentiality would have on organizational operations, organizational assets, or individuals.
1475 [FIPS 199]

1476 **Third-Party Relationships** - relationships with external entities. External entities may include,
1477 for example, service providers, vendors, supply-side partners, demand-side partners, alliances,
1478 consortiums, and investors, and may include both contractual and non-contractual parties.
1479 [DHS]

1480 **Third-party Providers -** Service providers, integrators, vendors, telecommunications, and
1481 infrastructure support that are external to the organization that operates the manufacturing
1482 system.
1483

1484 **Thresholds -** Values used to establish concrete decision points and operational control limits to
1485 trigger management action and response escalation.

Appendix C - References

1. Executive Order no. 13636, Improving Critical Infrastructure Cybersecurity, DCPD-201300091, February 12, 2013. https://www.govinfo.gov/app/details/FR-2013-02-19/2013-03915

2. National Institute of Standards and Technology (2014) Framework for Improving Critical Infrastructure Cybersecurity, Version 1.0. (National Institute of Standards and Technology, Gaithersburg, MD), February 12, 2014. https://doi.org/10.6028/NIST.CSWP.02122014

3. Stouffer KA, Lightman S, Pillitteri VY, Abrams M, Hahn A (2015) Guide to Industrial Control Systems (ICS) Security. (National Institute of Standards and Technology, Gaithersburg, MD), NIST Special Publication (SP) 800-82, Rev. 2. https://doi.org/10.6028/NIST.SP.800-82r2

4. Joint Task Force Transformation Initiative (2013) Security and Privacy Controls for Federal Information Systems and Organizations. (National Institute of Standards and Technology, Gaithersburg, MD), NIST Special Publication (SP) 800-53, Rev. 4, Includes updates as of January 22, 2015. https://doi.org/10.6028/NIST.SP.800-53r4

5. The International Society of Automation (2019) *ISA99, Industrial Automation and Control Systems Security*. Available at https://www.isa.org/isa99/.

6. National Cybersecurity & Communications Integration Center (NCCIC) - https://www.dhs.gov/national-cybersecurity-and-communications-integration-center.

7. U.S. Department of Homeland Security, National Cybersecurity and Communications Integration Center (NCCIC) (2019) *Cybersecurity and Infrastructure Security Agency -- Industrial Control Systems*. Available at https://ics-cert.us-cert.gov/.

8. Stouffer K, Zimmerman T, Tang CY, Lubell J, Cichonski J, McCarthy J (2017) Cybersecurity Framework Manufacturing Profile. (National Institute of Standards and Technology, Gaithersburg, MD), NIST Internal Report (NISTIR) 8183, Includes updates as of May 20, 2019. https://doi.org/10.6028/NIST.IR.8183

9. J. J. Downs and E. F. Vogel, A Plant-Wide Industrial Process Control Problem, Computers and Chemical Engineering, vol. 17, no. 3, pp. 245-255, 1993.

10. L. Ricker, Decentralized control of the Tennessee Eastman Challenge Process, Journal of Process Control, vol. 6, no. 4, pp. 205-221, 1996.

11. Zimmerman T (2017) Metrics and Key Performance Indicators for Robotic Cybersecurity Performance Analysis. (National Institute of Standards and Technology, Gaithersburg, MD), NIST Internal Report (NISTIR) 8177, Includes updates as of May 21, 2019. https://doi.org/10.6028/NIST.IR.8177

1532   12. Tang CY (2017) Key Performance Indicators for Process Control System Cybersecurity
1533   Performance Analysis. (National Institute of Standards and Technology, Gaithersburg,
1534   MD), NIST Internal Report (NISTIR) 8188, 2017. https://doi.org/10.6028/NIST.IR.8188

www.ingramcontent.com/pod-product-compliance
Lightning Source LLC
Chambersburg PA
CBHW050736180526
45159CB00003B/1250